SWAT

BATTLE TACTICS

Foremost, we wish to dedicate this book to our wives, Mary Cascio and Marianne McSweeney. We truly and deeply appreciate your support of our undertaking in writing this book.

A special dedication goes to all the brave, honest, and caring police officers who lay their lives on the line every day. Thank you!

SWAT

BATTLE TACTICS

HOW TO ORGANIZE,

TRAIN, AND EQUIP

A SWAT TEAM FOR

LAW ENFORCEMENT

OR SELF-DEFENSE

Pat Cascio
John McSweeney

Paladin Press
Boulder, Colorado

*SWAT Battle Tactics: How to Organize, Train, and Equip a
SWAT Team for Law Enforcement or Self-Defense*

by Pat Cascio and John McSweeney
Copyright © 1996 by Pat Cascio and John McSweeney

ISBN 0-87364-900-1
Printed in the United States of America

Published by Paladin Press®, a division of
Paladin Enterprises, Inc., P.O. Box 1307,
Boulder, Colorado 80306, USA.
(303) 443-7250

Chapter 6 originally appeared as "Small Unit Tactics" in the
June 1987 issue of *American Survival Guide*. Reprinted with permission.

Cover photo courtesy of Michael's of Oregon.

PALADIN, PALADIN PRESS, and the "horse head" design
are trademarks belonging to Paladin Enterprises and
registered in United States Patent and Trademark Office.

Direct inquiries and/or orders to the above address.

Neither the author nor the publisher assumes
any responsibility for the use or misuse of
information contained in this book.

CONTENTS

Introduction/1

Chapter 1
Team Selection/5

Chapter 2
Firearms Selection/13

Chapter 3
Chemical Weapons/25

Chapter 4
Hostage Negotiations/39

Chapter 5
Handling the Media/47

Chapter 6
Infantry Tactics/53

Chapter 7
Clearing Buildings/65

Chapter 8
It's a Bomb!/83

Chapter 9
Physical Conditioning/89

Chapter 10
Hand-to-Hand Combat/95

Conclusion/105

Appendix
Resources/107

INTRODUCTION

SWAT, ERT, REACT, Special Services—all police teams operating as specialized or highly trained units fall into the category we refer to as MOUT (Military Operations in Urban Terrain). Though many police departments are loathe to admit it, the military has been using these special tactics and weapons for decades. In the last 20 years or so, police departments have adopted many of these military tactics and modified them to suit the needs of their own special weapons and tactics units. Indeed, many law enforcement SWAT instructors come from a military infantry background. A good military company commander or platoon leader with an infantry background makes an instructor or leader in this law enforcement field. Because infantry tactics are the basis for all SWAT tactics, we have devoted an entire chapter to this topic.

Unfortunately, the inception of MOUT has led many police and security departments to replace regularly scheduled training with so-called "high-tech" equipment. Let's make this perfectly clear: *No amount of equipment will replace training (in tactical situations) on a regular basis!* The trend these days is to purchase all-black uniforms (a strong point of contention with the public) and high-tech weaponry and equipment and then to neglect honest (and hard) training that is essential when you have to deploy in a high-level threat situation. This is not to say that specialized equipment doesn't have its place in the scheme of things—it does—but it doesn't replace the training skills necessary to become a highly efficient and well-oiled team. We have trained police and security officers in MOUT (or SWAT if you prefer) over the years, only to see them neglect any regularly scheduled training programs after their initial training.

Many police departments believe that by purchasing specialized weapons (e.g., M16s, Uzis, laser sights) they have a SWAT team of sorts and, therefore, some type of advantage over the bad guys. This is dangerous thinking and can result in unnecessary risks and, oftentimes, deaths (both civilian and law enforcement). We want to believe that police departments have advanced beyond the "good ol' boys" network of past sheriff's departments, where Billy Bob was summoned to "take out" a barricaded suspect with his faithful hunting rifle, but what we're seeing today leads us to believe many departments still have a similar mentality.

What often happens is that when police departments get funds from the city council or federal government for the organization of a SWAT team, the first thing they do is purchase new weapons (when there's nothing wrong with the "old" ones), fancy uniforms, and every other high-tech piece of equipment they have seen or read about in some of the popular police magazines and catalogs. Training is then *secondary* in their eyes. Indeed, this is just the reverse of what should be done. The training should be of *primary* concern; only after a suitable training period and indoctrination should departments seriously consider purchasing specialized equipment. Work with the tools you have, and once you become proficient with them, move on to other weapons and equipment you may need.

Another important point is that your team will not be able to handle every situation that arises. Your team must know its limitations. Should your team face a scenario that is beyond its capabilites, it is best to try to contain the situation until assistance can be called in. It's not shameful to seek outside assistance. It would be disastrous to commit your team to a situation that is beyond its training and capabilities and have deaths occur as a result of it.

In this book, we will examine a number of topics that an average SWAT or MOUT team could encounter. Some topics will be familiar to you; others may not. We will, of course, deal with the various weaponry available as well as tactical situations and training, equipment, public relations, hostage negotiations, and a number of other equally important areas of interest to police and paramilitary officers interested in training in this specialty field. This book is only the first step and should *not* be considered the final or only word on the subject. There are a number of good books out there that cover training in this area.

Cross-training is to be encouraged during team training. Keep in mind, however, that not every team member needs to be cross-trained in every area. Not every team member needs to be trained as a locksmith, sniper/countersniper, team leader, entryman, or public relations officer. Each team member should train in a few areas and then hone those skills to the highest degree possible. Choose your areas of interest, but don't try to do it all or to be something you're not. It takes a special person to be a hostage negotiator, just as it takes someone special to take out an armed felon at 100 yards with a scoped rifle. High-risk entry is another area that calls for nerves of steel.

NOTE: Before we get any letters from female officers, we'd like to explain that when we use the terms *man* and *men* or the pronoun *he* and *his*, they are used in the generic sense. We have trained and worked with female officers in SWAT operations who are every bit as effective as their male counterparts. As a matter of fact, we don't know why more female officers are not involved in SWAT or MOUT operations.

CHAPTER 1

TEAM SELECTION

One of the most important aspects of any SWAT or MOUT team is the correct selection of the personnel who will serve on it.

SELECTION PROCESS

There are five steps in the selection process: announcement of an opening on the team, a thorough review of applicants, psychological testing, personal interviews, and completion of training.

Announcing the Opening

The first step in this process is the announcement of open recruitment throughout the department or unit. Under *no* circumstances should people who have not volunteered be assigned to a team. Every member should be a volunteer—no exceptions! Personnel who have simply been assigned to a SWAT or MOUT team won't have their hearts, minds, and bodies in the training process: they just won't give their all when the time comes for action.

Reviewing the Applicants

Obviously, not everyone who volunteers is suitable for this type of training and work, so your second step is a careful examination of volunteers' training, experience, personnel records, and reasons for wanting to join the team. You don't need a "Rambo" or "Lone Wolf McQuade" on your team. You absolutely have to operate as a team. That's why it's called a SWAT or MOUT *team* and not a SWAT or MOUT *individual.* Those who have demonstrated an unwillingness to work within the framework already laid out in your departmental or unit guidelines should be excluded from consideration.

Testing the Applicants

The third step, psychological testing, might not apply to all departments. Officers in charge of staffing teams for smaller departments and units are more familiar with all their officers, whereas in the larger departments (e.g., Chicago, Los Angeles, New York) administrators will not know all the officers involved in the application process and must weed out anyone unsuitable for high-risk operations. One of the best ways to do this is through psychological testing. This should *not* be used as the final measuring tool in the selection process. We have a low regard for psychologists who think they are more important to the selection process than they really are. There is something to be said, however, for the results of the tests they administer and what can be learned through the testing process. Therefore, psychological testing has its place.

Interviewing the Applicants

The fourth step is a personal interview with the applicant,

preferably before a selection board of unbiased members to avoid the "good ol' boys" selection process. You don't need anyone on your team just because he is a friend of the chief of police or someone's nephew.

Your selection board should include a minimum of three members, preferably five. Board members need not be team members, but it is advisable that at least one or two have background, training, or experience in law enforcement or the military. It is not uncommon to have officers from outside agencies or departments serve on the board to avoid any favoritism in the selection process. A majority vote should be necessary before anyone can be allowed to join the team.

The personal interviews help you evaluate the candidates and assess their reasons for wanting to join the team. One type you want to be screen out is the person looking to be a hero. Everyone wants to feel important and be held in high esteem, and some people might think that a position on a SWAT or MOUT team would provide this. After all, the movies always portray SWAT team members as heroes. Let's be honest, everyone (deep down inside) would like to be a hero and make the front page of the newspapers or the six o'clock news. You don't need people who are interested in individual glory, but rather who are willing to work together as a team for the betterment of everyone affected: the team, the department, the city, the public.

Completing the Training

Once an applicant has made it past the selection board, he isn't automatically on the team. The fifth, and final, step in the selection process is the applicant's successful completion of training. If an applicant has completed the training and contributed to the team's overall readiness, then he can be considered a team member.

We would also like to recommend here that rookies (i.e., first-year police officers) be excluded from MOUT teams. It is better that they get some real street experience and training their first year or two before they are exposed to any specialized training or high-risk operations. This is simply a preference on our part. Your department or unit will need to draw up guidelines and regulations to govern your team.

SELECTION GUIDELINES AND REGULATIONS

When you are drafting guidelines, there are several factors that must be considered.

Maturity
Maturity should be the number one factor when drawing up any guidelines. You don't need any "kids" (mentally) on your team. Remember, we discussed *teamwork* earlier. This may sound redundant, but it takes a mature individual to be a team member. This may sound a bit contradictory to talk about *individuals* and *teamwork* in the same context. But, in this case, they work together.

Physical Readiness
Physical readiness is a vital concern (we'll discuss this further in Chapter 9). You don't need someone on your team who is physically unable to carry out the mission. This isn't to say that everyone needs to be built like Superman. Find a happy medium. Physical training should be a part of every training exercise. Armed forces include physical training in their tactical exercises, and so should your SWAT or MOUT team.

Police officers should always be in good-to-excellent physical condition, but, sadly, most are not. We don't believe it is unreasonable for a team to work out once or twice a week after a shift for 15 to 20 minutes to stay in shape. Your tactical exercises will take a certain amount of physical strength to complete (if properly designed). Our combined experience in the martial arts spans better than

65 years, and we know that the "secret" to being physically fit is doing simple yoga-type exercises. We both perform
simple stretching exercises called Tiger Moves regularly.
These were developed by John McSweeney (more on this
in Chapter 9).

Any serious student of the martial arts will attest to the
fact that those who are the most limber are the ones who can
perform even the hardest moves, blocks, kicks, and so on.
Even limber people who are overweight can perform movements more easily than the skinny guys who don't have any
flexibility. Physical conditioning—don't neglect it; include it in
every training exercise.

Mental Conditioning

Another "secret" that experienced martial artists attempt
to instill in their students is the mental conditioning or mind-
set needed to win any deadly confrontation. Winning a fight
is about 20 percent physical and 80 percent mental, as our
good friend and fellow martial artist Bradley J. Steiner stress-
es regularly in his "Defensive Combat" column in Petersen's
Handguns magazine.

During your regular training exercises, focus on the mental conditioning of your team members as well. Someone
who is having personal, financial, or health problems is not
suitable for a high-risk operation. This is not to say he must
be dropped from the team. But you should exclude him from
a call-out or assign him to a nonthreatening position until the
problem can be resolved (remember cross-training?). You
don't need someone on your team pulling the trigger at the
wrong time because he is not 100 percent into the operation.
Everyone goes through bouts of depression. We don't care
who you are. Make observations and notes on your team
members and encourage them to discuss their problems with
you and seek professional help if it is indicated. Mental readiness: every team member must possess it.

TEAM ASSIGNMENTS

Another area that should be addressed in team selection is that of assignments. Some members are better suited to certain jobs than others. Someone with an infantry background might be an excellent choice for high-risk entry or room clearing, because he is already trained in this activity. Someone who has been a U.S. Marine may be an excellent candidate for a sniper/countersniper role because the Corps is known for turning out some of the best marksmen in the world. Someone with an investigative background might be suitable for collecting the intelligence necessary to carry out an operation successfully. Those experienced in public speaking might be perfect for handling the media and crisis reporting. Street supervisors might make excellent team leaders and training officers. There are a number of diverse functions involved in a full-scale call-out. During a real call-out you could use beat cops or reserve officers to clear innocents from their homes, but if they don't practice or train with your team on a regular basis, how are they going to know what to do? Make sure everyone who has (or might have) a role in a crisis is a member of the team and practices with it regularly. Don't forget.

How Many Members on a SWAT Team?
There is no such thing as a one- or two-man SWAT team. You need a minimum of five officers for a team to be effective. On a five-man team, one person is the team leader or supervisor, and the other four are the operational members. A six- or eight-member team is also workable. From this point on, personnel should be divided up into other teams. In a building-clearing operation, especially with a multistory building, more than one team will need to be deployed to clear the building effectively. Each team works separately yet together with the other teams involved, using radio communications or planned operations.

Once your team has been selected, it is important to break the members down into the various jobs they'll be performing. There are entry teams, negotiation teams, communication teams, intelligence officers, and so on. Again, seek out what positions your personnel are experienced or interested in. You can get a better feel for their particular qualifications and aptitude once regular training exercises begin. It is not a problem to reassign someone to a different job at a later date. Everyone should be placed and trained where they will be most effective.

Our friend and associate, James R. Jarrett, director of the United States Marksmanship Academy in Phoenix, Arizona, is a former Green Beret and former member of the Los Angeles Police Department's SWAT team and one of the finest instructors we know, a no-nonsense type of guy who doesn't believe in magic formulas or other such foolishness. We have our honest points of disagreement with him, but the one thing we do agree on is that too many SWAT team operations are what he calls "gee whiz" operations at best. Don't let this happen to your team. You know what he means: those units that have purchased the ninja suits with black hoods and a bunch of M16s or HK MP5 submachine guns and neglected any kind of regular training. Then, when they're called out to an emergency, the pros watch in amazement, shake their heads, and mutter disgustedly, "Gee whiz." And pity the poor souls they are supposed to rescue. Don't let this happen to your team.

CHAPTER 2

FIREARMS SELECTION

Today's weaponry is limited only by the imagination of the user—and we don't make this statement lightly. There is an endless array of handguns, rifles, shotguns, knives, and other weapons on the market. We won't go into extreme detail about the numerous firearms that can be used for today's SWAT, MOUT, or paramilitary team. We will, however, cover the more popular and usable firearms on the market. It should be noted that many of the highly trained and skilled SWAT teams today use slightly modified single-action autoloaders in .45 ACP. The FBI Hostage Rescue Team recently adapted a high-capacity .45 ACP autoloader based on the Para-Ordnance line of pistols, abandoning the Browning Hi-Power 9mm pistol. Coauthor Pat Cascio recently completed a book entitled *The*

Double-Action Dilemma (Vigilante Publishing, P.O. Box 592, Ontario, OR 97914, $22.95 plus $3.00 shipping) that covers many of today's top double-action and double-action-type autoloading pistols. His book goes into great detail regarding the good points as well as the bad ones on each gun tested and is worth reading if you are planning to buy a new double-action pistol.

HANDGUNS

Our recommendation for any SWAT, MOUT, or paramilitary team member is simply to use the gun you are most familiar with. Your duty handgun will serve you nicely. We know that the trend is toward whatever is newest on the market, but any good, serviceable duty handgun will suit your purposes as long as it is a minimum of 9mm or .38-Special caliber. Most will get the job done with the proper bullet and load. Must reading for any serious student of self-defense are Evan Marshall and Ed Sanow's seminal book on stopping power, *Handgun Stopping Power*, and its follow-up, *Street Stoppers* (both published by Paladin Press). Both are welcome additions to any law enforcement library.

When you are making high-risk entries or serving felony arrest warrants, a long gun may be too cumbersome to maneuver with any degree of ease. Further, it is a rare occasion, indeed, when your suspect is armed with anything other than a handgun. However, there is the "what if" scenario that is played out in every tactical situation, and you must be capable of responding accordingly. Obviously, a handgun is no match for a shotgun's stopping power at close quarters, nor is a shotgun any match for a semiautomatic rifle (at long ranges). Of course, if you have done your job and collected the proper intelligence, you will know beforehand what type of weapons your suspect is likely to be armed with.

Colt .45 ACP

Right up front, we'll confess that we are great fans of the .45 ACP Colt Government Model (and such clones as those

The Colt Government Model in .45 ACP is the perfect entry weapon and one of the authors' favorite guns.

Colt's new Double Eagle is available in .45 ACP, 10mm, and the new .40-caliber S&W.

made by Springfield Armory and Norinco) and would likely make this our first choice for duty carry, tactical operations, high-risk entries, felony arrests, or building searches. The unmatched and time-proven effectiveness of this gun-ammunition combination speaks for itself.

Colt recently released its Officers Model Double Eagle in .45 ACP, which we find balances in the hand like it was made to be there. This is an excellent concealed carry gun, but it performs just as well as the full-sized version. There is nothing wrong with the full-sized gun; however, those who tested both models preferred the smaller one by a big margin.

Sturm, Ruger Model P90

The newly released Sturm, Ruger and Company Model P90 .45 ACP is without doubt one of the finest pistols to come down the pike. It performed flawlessly right out of the box, feeding every kind of ammo we put through it. It is fairly light for its size; the slide is made of stainless steel, and its frame is lightweight aluminum alloy. The best news is that the gun retails for less than $450 and in our humble opinion is the best buy on the market in a double-action .45 ACP.

Springfield Armory and Taurus International

Springfield Armory and Taurus International are two of our favorite gun companies, and they both have excellent autoloaders on the market that fit the bill nicely. The recently released Springfield Armory Line Personal Defense Weapons (PDW) in .45 ACP should prove popular with knowledgeable police officers, as will the Taurus Model PT100 in .40-caliber S&W that is now on the market. With a handgun from either of these companies you can rest easy, knowing you are well armed.

Glock

The Glock line of autoloaders has taken the market by

Glock's Model 20 in 10mm should have plenty of power with a 15-round magazine.

storm over the past eight years. The company offers subcompact, compact, and full-sized 9mm and .40-caliber S&W pistols, as well as the superb 10mm and .45 ACP pistols. Overall, it has a pretty fantastic product that is worth looking into, but there are several shortcomings that we would like to see corrected on the Glocks. If you're going to use a Glock, take the time to train in the proper gun-handling procedures for this line of guns. Proper training in the use of any firearm is the key to the successful outcome of any lethal confrontation.

SHOTGUNS

We will not spend a lot of time covering shotguns in this book because reams have been written about the effectiveness of a shotgun. Chuck Karwan—a noted gun scribe, former Green Beret, and close friend—argues that shotguns have extremely limited use in modern police work, especially in tactical operations, and we agree.

First, they have a limited range, not much beyond 25 to

30 yards with double-ought buckshot and out to approximately 75 yards with a rifled slug. Most police departments don't spend the time (or money) necessary for their officers to become skilled marksmen with a shotgun (if there is any such thing as a marksman with a shotgun). Many police officers are not into guns per se and take offense at the recoil of a stout buckshot load. To get them to fire a sizable number of rounds on a regular basis is all but impossible. This is not to say that a shotgun doesn't have its place in general police work and SWAT team applications—it does. Used within its limitations, a shotgun performs well.

When a shotgun is carried in the patrol car and used against more than one armed suspect, the intimidation factor alone justifies its use. We would much rather have a shotgun in hand than a pistol when serving a felony arrest warrant. However, because of its length, a shotgun is difficult to maneuver anyplace other than in the wide-open spaces.

There are a number of good quality shotguns on the market today, far too many to list here. We tested two guns

Pat Cascio test-fires the new Mossberg Intimidator 590 shotgun with laser sight built in.

in particular while preparing this book, both worthy of a closer look.

Mossberg Model 590 Intimidator

The Mossberg Model 590 Intimidator, with a built-in laser sight in the forearm, is a solid choice in a pump-action shotgun. Light pressure on the forearm activates the laser sight that is zeroed for 12 yards. The gun performed flawlessly when tested by a sheriff's department.

Benelli M1 Super 90

A second gun that we evaluated was from Heckler & Koch, the Benelli M1 Super 90 in 12 gauge. This semiauto shotgun operates on the blowback principle rather than being gas operated, as is the Remington 1100. The gun came equipped with double-ought and slug loads, but would not function with any regularity using light field loads. To be honest, the gun was set up for police work and not for hunting. The only drawback to the Benelli is that the price is rather high and may be beyond the budget of smaller departments. However, either gun will serve you for many years without problems.

Before closing our discussion on shotguns, we would like to make a few more observations. We hate to see the word *accuracy* used when discussing shotguns. A handgun will outperform a shotgun in the accuracy department at any reasonable range when the shotgun is using double-ought loads. This term is totally inappropriate when referring to a shotgun's intended purpose. Many people envision the "riot gun" being shot into a crowd of unruly demonstrators or rioters and thus ending the riot. It simply doesn't happen that way, and, given its limited range, a shotgun can only be used within specific parameters. Although versatile in many ways, the shotgun would not be our first choice as a special operations weapon on a SWAT or MOUT operation. It is sometimes used as a security weapon in SWAT operations and by sniper teams.

Anyone who reads gun magazines will know that the shotgun is "recommended" as the perfect gun for defending a home or business. We seriously doubt that many of those who write these articles have ever taken the time to go through their own home with a shotgun. Had they done so, they would see how difficult it is to maneuver this long gun. Moreover, it is deafening to fire a shotgun within the confines of a room.

If you are clearing a large, mostly empty warehouse, a shotgun may come in handy. However, the long range may be a handicap. If you are assigned to guard the front or rear door or a window of a building, depending upon the range, the shotgun may be the perfect weapon, especially when more than one suspect may exit at once. It may sound like we're putting the shotgun down, but this is not the case. We just want you to be aware of its limitations.

RIFLES AND CARBINES

We like to refer to rifles and carbines as "special weapons" because they can perform any task a shotgun can—and better. The difference between a rifle and a carbine is that the carbine resembles a short-barreled rifle and normally shoots a less powerful cartridge.

More and more police departments are learning the following advantages of equipping their officers with rifles or carbines instead of shotguns: (1) The rifle can be used at longer ranges. (2) It has more power. (3) It has a higher magazine capacity (autoloaders). (4) It is easier to shoot. (5) In many cases, surplus ammunition for practice can be had at very low prices.

There is some argument about which rifle is best, bolt-action or semiautomatic. Though there is nothing wrong (mechanically) with the bolt-action rifle, the semiautomatic is easier to shoot (less recoil), and follow-up shots are faster.

The Eagle Arms Action Master is a superb urban sniper rifle.

The Eagle Arms H-BAR is an excellent all-around SWAT weapon.

This second reason alone is enough to choose an autoloader in our opinion. Additionally, many companies are now making police carbines that use handgun ammunition, and the prices are quite low.

One drawback to autoloaders is that they usually cost more than an out-of-the-box bolt rifle, and if your department is on a tight budget, this may be a determining factor (of course, police snipers generally do not use out-of-the-box bolt rifles). We are not talking about a rifle that is going to be issued as standard equipment, rather we are discussing the rifle in the role of sniper/countersniper weapon. Top-notch accuracy is needed for such an operation, so surplus weapons that can be purchased for less than $200 are not the topic of this discussion.

Eagle Arms

This fairly new company is turning out one of the best (if

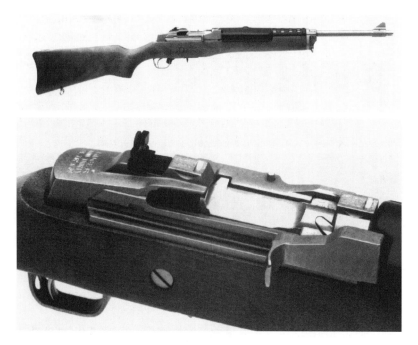

Ruger's new Mini-30 should prove to be an excellent entry weapon.

not *the* best) AR-15-style rifle/carbine in .223 caliber that we have run across. We recently tested three of its guns: the H-BAR, Carbine, and brand-new Action Master. Although the H-BAR would make an excellent all-around weapon, the little Carbine would make do as an entry weapon because of its size and ease of handling. The Action Master, though designed for the shooting sports, is best deployed in the role of a sniper/countersniper rifle. It is a match-grade rifle with a Douglas premium heavy barrel that will easily shoot half-inch groups at 100 yards with the right .223 Remington ammunition. This is more than accurate enough for any urban situations in which a sniper/countersniper may be deployed. Many would opt for a .308-caliber long gun instead of the .223, but we believe that the smaller caliber is much better suited for the urban terrain. There is less likelihood of overpenetration, thus reducing the chance of innocent civilians being hit.

Sturm, Ruger and Company

Sturm, Ruger and Company produces two very fine rifles in its Mini-14 and Mini-30 guns. The Mini-14 fires the .223 round, and the Mini-30 fires the 7.62x39mm round. We believe that both of these little guns would make excellent entry or rear-guard weapons because of their short overall length. The 7.62x39mm round proved much more accurate than the .223 Remington. Chuck Karwan confirmed to coauthor Pat Cascio that the 7.62x39 round will indeed outshoot the .223 Remington in a *properly barreled gun*. The recent imported military surplus rifles arriving from China simply do not possess the accuracy the 7.62x39 round is capable of delivering. In a side-by-side test, the Mini-30 did indeed outshoot the Mini-14.

We do not believe that either of these Rugers is capable of match-grade accuracy; however, both are capable of being employed in a sniper/countersniper role of less than 100 yards with the right ammunition and a good scope. They best serve as entry weapons or for securing the outer perimeters of a building because they have plenty of knockdown power, much more than a handgun can provide.

Heckler & Koch

Heckler & Koch is well known for its outstanding line of handguns, shotguns, and submachine guns. The submachine gun to have (if your team deems one necessary) is the fine HK MP5 9mm. The FBI, U.S. Secret Service, and every other knowledgeable SWAT team in the world agree: there is no better submachine gun for close-quarter combat.

However, keep in mind that many hours of practice must go into the effective use of any submachine gun. If your chances of employing such a firearm is extremely remote, then we suggest that you spend your training funds elsewhere.

We would like to reemphasize one point in closing here: our purpose in writing this book was not to cover weapons in any great detail. This is not a book about shooting, but rather one about tactics, training, and team selection for SWAT teams. Every police department has its own set of circumstances, terrain, budgetary constraints, and training programs that will dictate what will work for it and what won't. Draw up all the possible scenarios that you believe your team may encounter and then decide what equipment is needed and what you can afford. As already mentioned, no amount of high-tech gear or weapons will replace training. Make training your number-one priority.

CHAPTER 3

CHEMICAL WEAPONS

Chemical warfare has been around since 1912, when the police in Paris, France, first used "hand bombs" with an early type of tear gas. However, chemical munitions were not widely used until World War I when all sides involved in this global conflict used them. Many deadly chemical munitions were developed during this period, none of which are suitable for deployment by law enforcement agencies.

CHOOSING A CHEMICAL AGENT

There are two types of agents available to law enforcement agencies for riot or crowd control as well as limited use against barricaded suspects. Both chloroacetophenone (CN) and orthochlorbenzalamalonoitrile (CS), are lacrimators (or tear-producing).

CN

CN was formerly the most widely used incapacitating agent. It was invented by a German chemist around 1869. It irritates the upper respiratory system and eyes, causing a heavy flow of tears seconds after exposure. In high concentrations, CN irritates the skin and causes a burning sensation, and it may produce nausea in some individuals. However, many individuals are not affected by CN, and on them the agent may fail to produce the desired effect (that being retreat or surrender). Another drawback to CN is that it is usually dispensed by burning and delivered by hand grenades or launched projectiles, which could produce dangerous fires.

One of the best ways to dispense CN is through the fogging devices now being used by large law enforcement agencies. However, these units are expensive and most likely out of the reach of all but the largest departments. The fogger is especially useful when trying to disperse large crowds or rioters. The visual effect alone is sometimes enough to send rioters running for cover.

CS

CS was developed in 1928. Until 1961, when the British used it to control civil disorders on Cyprus, CS was used mainly within military circles. These days, it is common to find National Guard units equipped solely with CS. One drawback, as discovered by Col. Rex Applegate, is that many of the supplies of CS now in stock with National Guard and active army units are past their expiration date and may be inert. The munitions now on hand should be used for training purposes and replaced with current, updated supplies.

Tests conducted by physicians and toxicologists have indicated that the probability of lasting effects or death from exposure to CS is extremely low if it is properly used in riot-control situations. However, let us point out that the definitive

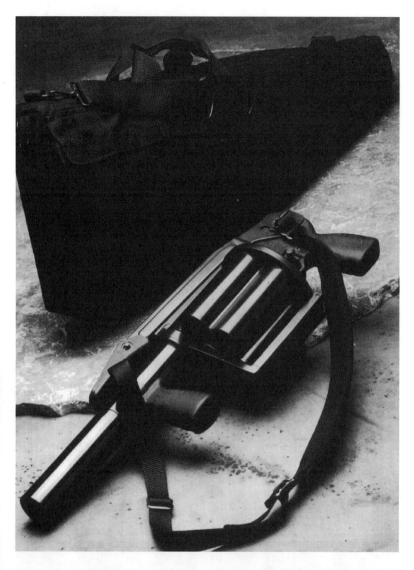

Federal Labs Model L-6 37/38mm multilauncher will get your chemical munitions on target.

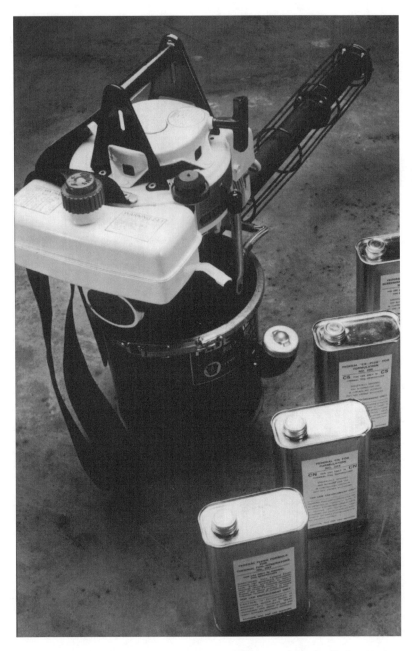

A fogger should come in handy during riots. This model is by Federal Labs.

When deploying chemical weapons, always be aware of the fire hazard. Don't cause another Waco!

words are *probability and properly.* You should keep them in mind, along with the now too-often-used word, *liability.* As the BATF raid on the Branch Davidians in Waco, Texas, and the subsequent FBI-ordered gassing so tragically demonstrated, there is *always* the chance that death can result when chemicals are used, and your decision to use chemical agents should take this into consideration.

USING CHEMICAL AGENTS

Once you have determined which chemical agent to use, you need to learn how to use them. There are any number of good schools that teach the proper deployment of chemical munitions, and most of them will certify you in the use of these weapons and munitions after you've successfully completed their training. We have no problem with training—after all, that is one of the reasons for this book, and we're sure you wouldn't be reading this book if you weren't interested in getting the proper training. However, the certification is only as good as the particular training institution that issued it. Being certified by a school doesn't mean much in some circles.

With the above in mind, we would like to recommend one particular school for chemical weapons and munitions training, Def-Tec Corporation (2399 Forman Road, Rock Creek, OH 44084-0208). Def-Tec is one of the leaders in chemical weapon and munitions training and is recognized by most of the major law enforcement departments in the United States. One word of warning: you will not only be taught how to deploy chemical munitions, you will also be exposed to them. You'll know what it feels like to be on the receiving end.

Having warned you about the dangers of chemical agents and strongly recommended specialized training—at Def-Tec, if possible—we will outline some principles on the proper deployment of chemical agents in a SWAT operation for those of you who are unable to afford to go away for extended training.

Barricaded Suspects or Snipers

One particular situation you are likely to encounter is that of the barricaded suspect or the sniper. When the suspect is in a house or building, it is important to isolate him and make his movement from room to room impossible. The layout of the building (i.e., whether it is a single-story or multistory dwelling or warehouse) will dictate how you employ your chemical agents. If, for example, you are dealing with a lone suspect in a one-story, single-family home, the recognized use of chemical munitions is to fire your projectile into adjoining rooms before firing them into the room the suspect is in.

By doing this, you will effectively prevent the suspect from moving from room to room to escape the gas. Once the gas has been deployed, allow enough time for the agent to permeate the room. If the suspect does not emerge, it should be assumed that he has either lost consciousness, moved to another room, or used a chemical or gas mask. If you have done your homework and collected the necessary intelligence, you should know if the suspect is armed with a gas mask. Nothing constructive is gained by firing additional rounds into the building at this point.

Once a chemical attack is under way, the SWAT team leader or commander should maneuver his team to gain a more advantageous field or assault position. At this point, it should be noted that the use of chemical munitions should be considered a part of the operation and an isolated phase during which other activities cease. Far too often we've observed law enforcement officers using chemical munitions solely as a means to end a confrontation rather than as an integral part of the full operation. Remember "gee whiz" operations? You *must* coordinate your entire operation; this means having proper communications or planned operations.

Entering Multistory Structures

Another situation you may encounter is that of deploying chemical agents in a multifamily dwelling or building. In this case, depending upon where the suspect is, you may want to employ chemical agents in the upper floors first (if the suspect is on a lower floor). By doing this, you will have effectively blocked his retreat to upper floors. Then, you would disperse your agents as outlined above (i.e., adjoining rooms first, etc.).

It is important not to use pyrotechnic devices in any situations where the risk of fire is unacceptable (remember Waco?). Even some expulsion devices can cause fires.

If you are using chemical agents, you need a gas mask. Federal Labs Model 6006 should do the job.

Whenever you are using chemical agents, it is advisable to have the fire department standing by—at a safe distance.

One of the leaders in the production of chemical agents and weapons is Federal Laboratories (P.O. Box 305, Saltsburg, PA 15681-0305). Although there are a number of

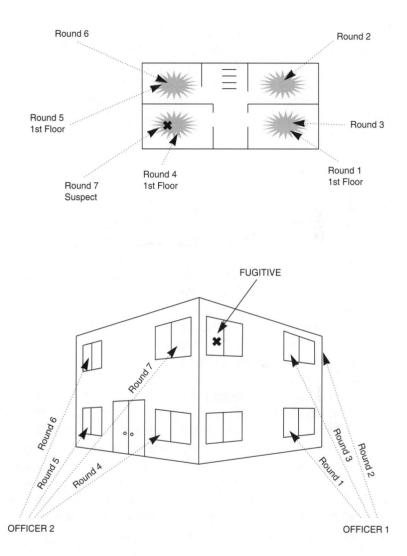

Round 6

Round 2

Round 5
1st Floor

Round 3

Round 7
Suspect

Round 4
1st Floor

Round 1
1st Floor

FUGITIVE

Round 7

Round 6

Round 5

Round 4

Round 3

Round 1

Round 2

OFFICER 2

OFFICER 1

You should deploy chemical weapons in the surrounding rooms before using them in the room the suspect is in in order to prevent his movement to other rooms.

chemical munitions companies around, we suggest that you order Federal's newest catalog. It is filled with the latest and most up-to-date munitions and weapons available.

A few more thoughts prior to closing our discussion on chemical agents. At the start of this book, we mentioned that no amount of high-tech gear, weapons, or equipment could substitute for training in preparing a SWAT team. Over the years, many police departments have gone overboard in the purchase of chemical munitions and weapons. Unless you are a large metropolitan police department, you can get by with the minimum amount of equipment.

In the course of training smaller police departments, we've had the chance to use various types of chemical agents, including tear gas grenades, foggers, and launched projectiles. It is simply amazing how quickly a single 12-gauge tear gas round will clear out a room full of hardened, experienced cops. So, with this in mind, bigger and more isn't necessarily better in this case. Remember, most chemical munitions have a limited shelf life and must be used within their specified time frame to be effective. No need to go overboard and purchase more than you can possibly use.

Although a SWAT team may be called out to serve in a riot or crowd-control situation, it should be stressed that as many team members as possible should be trained in the proper use and deployment of chemical agents. The best book on the subject of riot and crowd control is *Kill or Get Killed* by Col. Rex Applegate (available from Paladin Press). This classic text belongs in every serious law enforcement and military library. With that recommendation, we'll close this chapter and let you get on with training.

Federal Laboratories has an excellent selection of CN and CS hand grenades.

Smoke grenades, such as these from Federal Labs, will cover your team's movement.

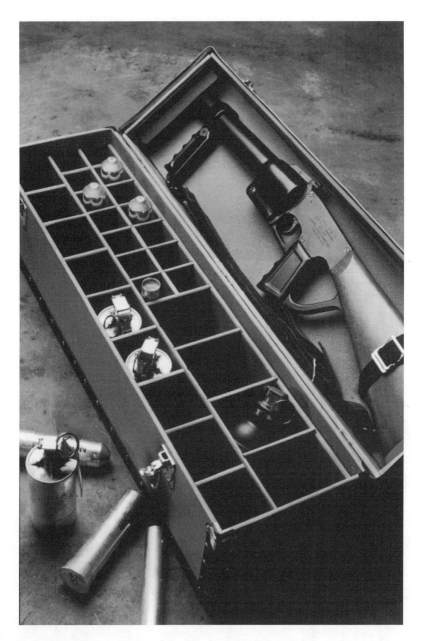

With this Model 204 gas gun from Federal Labs, you can "reach out and touch someone."

CHAPTER 4

HOSTAGE NEGOTIATIONS

The police negotiator, although oftentimes behind the scene, plays a most important role in every hostage situation. Life-and-death decisions hang in the balance during communications between the hostage taker (HT) and the police negotiator (PN). One wrong word or a word spoken in anger by a negotiator can cost innocent people their lives. Stress, emotions, and physical and mental anxiety are at their highest in the opening minutes of the hostage situation. Psychologists refer to it as the "cornered-rat syndrome." Everything possible must be done to alleviate the stress and pressure of this condition as soon as possible. Many times, a patrol officer is on the scene first and is unwillingly thrust into the position of PN. This is but one reason every officer should be grounded in the basics of negotiations.

Large metropolitan police departments will probably have a good number of trained negotiators on the scene in a matter of minutes. Small or rural departments don't have this luxury and must depend on whoever may be on the scene.

We strongly advocate role playing as a major part of active PN training. However, this is not the only training recommended for officers. A good public speaking course is helpful because it exposes an officer to speaking with and to strangers, and it also encourages proper diction. Diction is important, because certain words may sound alike but mean something entirely different. A wrong word can cost a life. When dealing with the HT, the PN will be involved primarily in question-and-answer communications, so it is good practice to speak publicly as often as possible and to take questions from the audience. This is one reason broadcasting courses are encouraged as part of your training. We know a number of radio disc jockeys (or radio personalities as they are now called), and they are trained to have an easy-going, relaxed attitude when they are on the air. Listeners or callers are immediately put at ease by the DJ. Think about it: this is exactly what the PN needs to do with the HT—relieve the pressure and stress of the situation as soon as possible.

As already mentioned, role playing is an important part of your training. Get other officers or civilian volunteers (screen them carefully) to play the part of the HT. Plan out the scene in advance with your volunteers. Will the communications between the PN and the HT take place over the phone, through a locked door or open window, or in a vehicle? Was a bank just robbed or a roomful of schoolchildren taken hostage? Is the HT mentally disturbed or a barricaded suspect? Take scenarios from today's headlines or look through your old files and play the scenes out. One note of caution: many times officers in role playing tend to forget that this is a training class for a life-or-death situation that may occur and tend to get just a bit lighthearted. This is to be corrected at once. Stress the importance of this type of training. Have the necessary props on hand for your session, for example, phones, doors, curtains, windows, tape recorders (be careful here), notepads, coffee, and sandwiches. To be an effective PN you must combine the qualities and traits of a salesman, actor, cleric, psychologist, mother, father, brother, sister. Spend time studying people in these roles. Observe how they handle situations, and take plenty of notes.

The job of a PN is both mentally and physically demanding and may go on for several hours or days. One of the traits of a good PN is an attitude of *sincerely* wanting to help. Notice that we emphasize *sincerely*. If the HT gets the impression that you are only acting or that you don't give a damn about him and are only concerned with the hostages' welfare, he will be suspicious of anything else you might say or do. Establish your sincerity at the outset. Let the HT know you are there to *help him*. If you can't, you will have a tough row to hoe.

Let the HT believe he is in control of the situation so he won't feel helpless or cornered. When an HT makes unreasonable demands, don't necessarily turn them down immediately. Remember, you are trying to buy time and defuse the situation. Establish key phrases such as, "I'll see what I can do," or "I know my supervisor won't go for it, but I'll do my best for you."

As far as promises go—don't make any you can't keep. Make it clear to the HT that you are only the go-between and anything outside of departmental policy or procedures must be cleared by someone higher up than yourself. And although you must come across as being flexible to a certain degree, don't give the HT anything without getting something in return. Bargain with him.

An often overlooked attribute for a hostage negotiator is fluency in more than one language. In the United States, Spanish is an excellent second language. In other parts of the world, it is worthwhile to speak and understand French. When learning another language, you should study the customs and culture of the country as well as the words. What may mean one thing in American slang, may mean an entirely different thing in another culture, even among English-speaking countries. This amusing anecdote from a friend of Pat's illustrates this point. One of Pat's American friends is married to a lovely lady from England. One day, a delivery person knocked on their door and tried to deliver a package to the husband. The husband wasn't home, and his wife wanted the delivery person to come back the next day when her husband would be home and knock on the door. However, what she said was, "My husband isn't home. Come back tomorrow morning and knock me up." We can only imagine what the delivery driver must have thought. So it is important to choose your words carefully.

In training police officers in negotiation techniques, we have found that men and women can serve equally well in the role of PN, with certain exceptions. First of all, it is important to try and match the PN to the HT. One of the problems female negotiators run into is the HT making obscene or perverted sexual comments to them. On more than one occasion, we've seen female officers go to pieces during role playing when an actor on the other end of the phone suggested some type of sexual fantasy or act. If you are a female PN or plan to be one, make sure that you are aware of signs that the situation is starting to break down or that the HT is becoming obsessed with you. Speak with the authority of your position and make it clear to the HT that you are a professional and that you are there to help him.

One last point before going on is that only one PN should communicate with the HT at a time. Don't let the HT play one against the other as children often do with parents. We are all different, and the HT may be shopping for a better deal if more than one PN is involved.

NEGOTIATION GUIDELINES

There are a number of guidelines to be followed when dealing with an HT. Two cardinal rules are the following: (1) Police officers or police negotiators are not traded for hostages. (2) The PN must not expose himself to the HT. Initial negotiations should (if at all possible) take place from a protected position. Don't expose yourself to gunfire or other danger needlessly.

As mentioned earlier, you are there to help. Once lines of communication are established with the suspect, the first thing out of your mouth should be, "I am the police negotiator. How can I help you?" By doing this, you are identifying yourself and offering to help the suspect. At times, this is all that is needed to get the suspect to surrender. Many HTs are thrust into this position by sheer stupidity, bad luck, or a plan (or no plan) gone wrong. They want assurance that the police are not going to kill them.

If the HT is serious about surrendering, there are two avenues of approach. The suspect can release all hostages and then come out, or the HT can merely throw his weapons out and come out himself, leaving the hostages inside. Of the two, the former is preferable in case the HT has a change of heart and gunfire erupts. Caution must be exercised when "hostages" are released. Each hostage must be suspected of being the HT. The hostages must be escorted away from the scene ASAP, searched, detained (if not in need of medical care), and interrogated. One point to keep in mind is that there are no guarantees in a hostage situation. Expect the best, but plan for the worst.

If an HT refuses to surrender, the negotiation process must begin. You will find that most HTs will immediately start making demands. This must be played down, and you need to start collecting intelligence information to be used in alternative plans. One of the best ways to do this is by telling the

If a police negotiator is to meet a hostage taker face-to-face, it should be under the watchful eye of a police sniper.

HT you want to get to know him. This will establish your sincere interest in him and his predicament, and it will also help defuse the situation by buying time for the hostages and for your tactical team to assess the situation. It is amazing how stupid most criminals are—the HT may tell you his entire family history.

CIVILIAN NEGOTIATORS

Conventional wisdom was to avoid them like the plague, but law-enforcement agencies, including the FBI, are now beginning to rethink this position. I know, we have all seen movies where a kindly father, reverend, cousin, wife, or

_____ (fill in the blank) has talked a suspect into surrendering. But it just doesn't happen this way in real life. For all you know, it may be that same person who caused the HT to react the way he did in the first place.

More than one person has been planted in the cemetery because of another person's good intentions. If, for whatever reason, a civilian negotiator is brought in, his intent must be thoroughly investigated—prior to allowing any type of communication with the HT.

DEADLINES

Avoid any kind of deadlines, which only serve to add to the pressure and stress of a crisis. If the HT pushes for a deadline and it arrives without compliance on your part, play it down and remind the HT that you never agreed to any such deadline. Additionally, give minimal attention and concern to the hostages. The Israelis and Germans have a policy that the hostages' safety is secondary, and this fact is well known to the terrorists of the world. Americans are more softhearted in this respect and have always shown too much concern for the safety of the hostages. To be sure, we are (and should be) concerned, but we don't have to express it openly! Many HTs—and especially terrorists—interpret such concern as a sign of weakness and use it to their advantage by making either real or imagined threats against the hostages' well-being. Play it down. Use key phrases such as, "Is anybody hurt in there?" This is directed at both hostages and the HT. You are honestly concerned with *everyone's* health and well-being. Honesty goes a long way in establishing good rapport with the HT.

AVOID ADDITIONAL HOSTAGES

We believe this next point is obvious, but for those new

to the law enforcement field, we want to state it just the same: *Refuse any demands for additional hostages.*

Under certain circumstances, face-to-face negotiations may occur. When they do, a few guidelines are in order. We believe, foremost, that you must make the HT "promise" not to hurt you or point a weapon at you. This is a reasonable demand on your part, one with which the HT should be willing to comply. Make any face-to-face meeting one-on-one and, if possible, arrange the meeting so you can be under the protective watch of a countersniper team. Never meet more than one HT face-to-face; otherwise, you are in jeopardy of being taken hostage yourself. Attempt to leave yourself an escape route in the event things take a bad turn. Never turn your back on the suspect and try to maintain eye contact. Don't make any sudden moves that may be construed as aggressive and, last, stay out of the suspect's immediate reach.

By following the steps outlined in this chapter, you may come to the point where you'll be able to give the HT orders. However, there will also come a point where a command decision must be made and further negotiations will only be a cover for a tactical response. In any event, be prepared for a long, drawn-out process.

CHAPTER 5

HANDLING THE MEDIA

Today, more than ever, a SWAT, MOUT, or paramilitary team must face the fact that sooner or later it will have contact with the media. With the advent of portable satellite dishes, law enforcement and military personnel are having to deal with the media, like it or not.

One of the often overlooked duties of a SWAT team call-out for any type of emergency or crisis is the responsibility for reporting facts to the media. The *T* in *SWAT* stands for tactics. One important tactic is handling the media in an orderly and effective manner.

All news reporting is slanted to some degree. Give any news network 30 minutes, and it'll make the news fit its agenda. Many of the weekly so-called "news magazines" go out and actually "create" the news they're presenting to viewers. Some are honestly no better than tabloids at the grocery checkout stands. Even the best of them often willfully slant their reporting to a greater degree than regular daily news programs.

How does the above relate to law enforcement? A SWAT call-out or paramilitary operation—whether it is for a riot, hostage situation, barricaded suspect, bombing, hijacking, felony arrest warrant, war, or whatever—will draw media attention from the local press and, in many situations, from national or international media. It is important to have a workable plan for dealing with the media so maybe they'll be working for you—or at least not against you.

The news media, in all honesty, are interested in the facts and not rumors. If your agency or unit provides the necessary facts in a precise, timely, and accurate manner, most media will report them. But if you do not, many will resort to reporting any rumors they hear or the "facts" as they see or interpret them.

The stress and pressure of a crisis can be reduced by planning the types of information you will release in a crisis. This must be done as a team effort, including your public relations officer, chief of police, district attorney, commanding officer, or any other units or agencies involved in the crisis. Because this is a team effort, you *must speak with one voice*, especially when several different law enforcement agencies are involved. This point was driven home to us recently while watching a news conference on Cable News Network (CNN) about serial murders of university students in Florida. Spokesmen for the agencies involved did not speak with one voice, nor were the officers involved in the conference prepared to respond to such typical questions from the media as who, what, where, when, why, and how. It made for a very sorry news conference on the part of the law enforcement community. Have answers to these six questions before scheduling any news conferences.

Of course, common sense must dictate what information will be released. Obviously, you never give information that may hurt your operation. In the past, the media have been instrumental in aiding law enforcement and military units by positioning their cameras so as not to reveal ongoing operations, investigations, etc. Keep in mind that this was a result of developing honest, cooperative relationships with the media before the crisis erupted.

There are no tricks involved when dealing with the media or the public in general—just be honest and fair and remember that the public has a legitimate interest in emergencies or life-threatening cases.

When dealing with a crisis, speed is important. Your team must coordinate and sometimes direct public relations with the news media. For example, say an officer is killed in the line of duty. It is important that you work with the public relations department and the media prior to reporting the officer's death. It would be an added trauma for the family of the slain officer to discover the death while viewing the evening news or to have a pool of reporters on their doorstep before being notified of the death through official channels. Special notifications need to be given first priority in certain situations.

Prior to any news conference, a press release should be compiled with all pertinent information and distributed to members of the media. This will often prevent your spokesmen from having to answer the same questions over and over. With today's technology, there is no excuse not to have press releases for all members of the media.

Notifying the press in a given order of preference should be considered as well. However, it seems that news cameras are often on the scene as rapidly as responding officers. If it is decided that the media is to be notified, it should be done in this order: local radio, local TV, daily newspapers, weekly newspapers, and then any other media. When the emergency is of national interest, the national wire services (e.g.,

Associated Press) should be notified first. When an emergency arises, it is too late to look up these phone numbers. Do it beforehand and establish contacts in these agencies.

There is a big difference between public relations and publicity. *Public relations* is the effort to inform the public about a specific situation, event, agency, or person, and to engender good will toward it. *Publicity* is merely having the situation, event, agency, or person made known to the public. Publicity can be either good or bad. A police officer who kills a felon in the line of duty produces good publicity. If an officer kills an innocent child, that means bad publicity. The goal of your public relations effort is to generate good publicity and to avoid or downplay bad publicity. Generally, a bad situation can be made even worse by ignoring the press or hampering their efforts. A situation can be turned into a disaster by attempting a cover-up.

Keep an information log. It helps keep track of the questions in an emergency. It can also control rumors before they spread or, if rumor control fails, to trace them afterward. A public information officer should be appointed to record all the information required in this log. A sample log is provided below.

As with any business, police department, and military or paramilitary unit, there is an all-important chain of command to be followed. Make sure that everyone knows and understands the chain prior to any crisis or operation. This will make referrals easier and more effective. A sample chain of command is shown on on page 51.

INFORMATION LOG

Date	Time	Subject of Inquiry or Rumor	Person Requesting Information, Tel #	Action Taken or Referrals

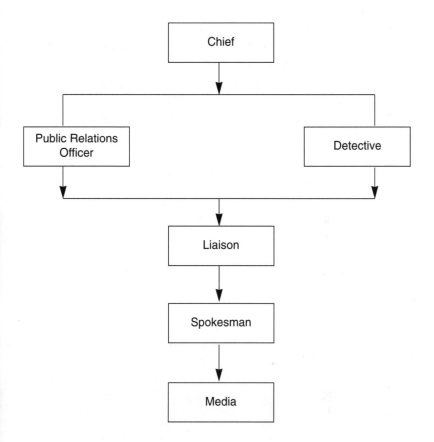

PROPER CHAIN OF COMMAND

Liaison activities should be set up wherever a contingency plan calls for it. The job of the liaison should be to contact appropriate local, state, county, or federal law enforcement agencies if needed. Also, fire and rescue units may be needed as well as such volunteer services as the Red Cross or Salvation Army (as was the case in the fire in Oakland, California). On long-term call-outs, hot coffee, donuts, sandwiches, rations, or meals ready to eat (MREs) are necessary.

Telephone and utility companies may be needed from time to time, and it is vitally important to have emergency phone numbers and contacts with these agencies.

The suggestions provided in this chapter are just basic guidelines for law enforcement, military, and paramilitary units to follow. You must adjust and incorporate your own policies and regulations when dealing with the media.

CHAPTER 6

INFANTRY TACTICS[1]

The rural sheriff's department or paramilitary unit has a different set of circumstances and battle tactics than the urban law enforcement or paramilitary unit. Such factors as terrain, distances involved (to engagement), weaponry, tactical considerations, communications (or lack thereof), and any number of other variables must be dealt with differently in the case of small agencies.

Small-unit infantry tactics are called for when dealing in open terrain (such as one might encounter in a wooded area, ranch, or farm). The information in this chapter is geared toward platoon- and squad-sized paramilitary units. SWAT, MOUT, or paramilitary teams can easily adapt this information to suit their particular needs and training agendas.

[1]This chapter first appeared as "Small Unit Tactics" in the June 1987 issue of *American Survival Guide*. Reprinted with permission.

With that said, sit back and enjoy a complete course in small-unit tactics that are suitable for law enforcement and paramilitary engagements and training exercises.

"The control of a large force is the same in principle as the control of a few men; it is merely a question of dividing up their numbers. Fighting with a large army under your command is nowise different from fighting with a small one. It is merely a question of instituting signs and signals." So wrote the Chinese General Sun Tzu in *The Art of War* some 500 years before the birth of Christ.

The basic unit of an army is the rifle squad. It consists of two fire teams and the squad leader. Each team consists of five men, one of whom is the team leader. Although there are eleven men in the squad, only two report to its leader and only four report to each fire team leader. This arrangement continues unbroken right up the ranks, normally with no more than four to five combat leaders reporting to anyone, including the commander in chief.

In the "triangular" organizational system favored by armies of the past and present, three rifle squads form a platoon, three rifle platoons a company, three rifle companies an infantry battalion, three battalions an infantry regiment, and three regiments an infantry division. In an infantry division, all crew-served weapons—including machine guns, mortars, armor, and artillery—are structured as separate units for training and maintenance purposes but in actual combat are assigned to rifle units either directly, as in the case of machine guns, or in support, as with artillery. In spite of all the manpower and material suddenly thrust upon the rifle units for direction and control, each infantry leader from squad to regiment finds he is burdened with only one or two more persons reporting to him. Thus, the span-of-control principle is maintained and the genius of Sun Tzu confirmed.

Armies at war maintain order of battle maps showing dispositions and deployment of enemy forces. The smallest tac-

A PLATOON ON THE MARCH

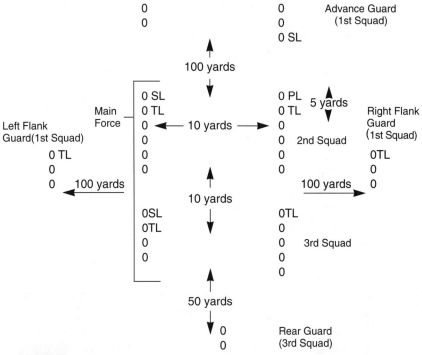

LEGEND

PL = Platoon Leader
SL = Squad Leader
TL = Team Leader
0 = Rifleman

The platoon leader is in visual contact with his three squad leaders and thus can issue hand commands (signals). Practice forming a line from this column until it becomes second nature for all members. The second squad moves to the left of the first squad while the third squad moves to the right. Flank guards move to the center to join the first squad, as does the platoon leader. During withdrawal, increase the rear guard to five men and reduce the advance guard to two men. Use 10-yard spacing between columns and 5-yard spacing between each individual.

PLATOON BATTLE LINE FORMATION

Battle Line

```
0 0 0 0 0 0 0 0 0 0 0 0 0 0 0 0 0 0 0 0 0 0 0 0 0 0 0 0 0 0 0 0
 0     TL     TL  SL      TL   SL  TL      SL  TL       TL    0
 0                                                            0
```

2nd Squad	0 PL	3rd Squad
	1st Squad	

LEGEND

PL = Platoon Leader
SL = Squad Leader
TL = Team Leader
0 = Rifleman

tical unit shown on such maps is the infantry battalion. Generals need to think in broad sweeps, and infantry battalions form a handy yardstick for rapid assessment.

For paramilitary purposes, our concern is small units, namely squads and platoons. They will normally operate alone with no supporting air, armor, or artillery and even without machine guns and mortars. If we learn to handle them well, then handling larger units should not be difficult, because the same tactical principles apply.

What are tactics? How do tactics differ from strategy? Our definitions, which, incidentally, don't come from any textbook, are as follows. *Strategy* is nothing more than the overall plan, and *tactics* are simply the optimum use of weapons. The Roman army used the close-ranked phalanx, with men standing one pace apart, because their main weapon was a 2-foot, blunt-edged stabbing sword. Modern armies disperse their riflemen at least 5 yards apart to minimize casualties. The Roman army fought hand-to-hand as a standard practice, something rare for a modern army because of the awesome firepower available.

Although weather, enemy, and terrain are important tactical considerations, the *weapon* is the distinguishing element and the essential cause of variations in tactics over the course of history.

WEAPONS

Paramilitary units should be armed with parts interchangability and ammunition resupply firmly in mind. We recommend that each rifleman be armed with a .223 semiautomatic rifle, .45-caliber semiautomatic pistol, and smoke, tear gas, and flash bang hand grenades. Team, squad, and platoon leaders should be armed exactly as the riflemen, and everyone must carry an entrenching tool.

Units must train to operate as independent-unit foot soldiers; therefore, all crew-served weapons are excluded because of their supply and transport requirements. There will be no support services; supplies are limited to what each man can carry on his back. Supply caches of food, water, medicine, and ammunition should be maintained within the anticipated operational area of each unit.

TACTICS

We will cover three basic types of tactics: march, offensive, and defensive.

March Tactics

March tactics are used in approaches to contact the enemy, to withdraw from the enemy, or merely to range over an area as a screening force.

Think of infantry war as a T. You move in a column and fight in a line. Move in columns of two with each man 5 yards behind the other and each column 5 to 10 yards apart.

Spacing will vary depending on the terrain and time of day. In jungles, dense woods, or nighttime operations, spacing could be as close as 1 yard. In open country during daylight hours, spacing could be 5 to 10 yards or even beyond, but the greater the spacing, the harder it is to control your men.

A platoon on the march should use advance, flank, and rear guards to protect the main force. An independently operating squad lacks the manpower for such guards. Instead, lead men watch the front, center men watch the flanks, and rear men watch the rear. Never permit men to straggle during a march. The men must be trained to keep a moderate pace, and with 10-minute rests every hour they should be able to march at least 10 hours a day. Guards must be posted for protection during night encampments. Guards should not stand or walk their posts, because this makes them easy targets for infiltrators. Instead, they should sit in locations offering maximum cover and concealment as well as a good overall field of vision. Rotate guards every two hours to minimize the tendency to fall asleep from fatigue.

If contact with the enemy is made during a march, the unit leader must decide on one of three courses of action to take: withdraw, attack, or defend.

RIFLE SQUAD ORGANIZATION

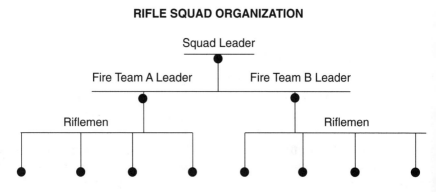

Offensive Tactics

The rifle squad attacks using fire and movement or fire and maneuver. One team becomes the base of fire and

FIRE AND MOVEMENT

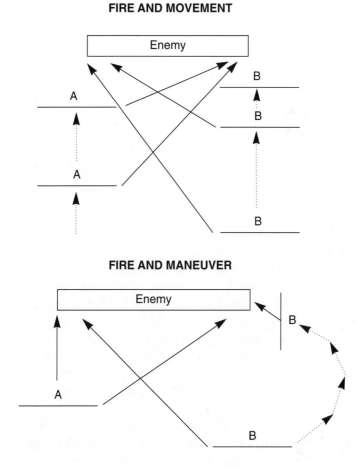

FIRE AND MANEUVER

Solid lines indicate the direction of fire. Dotted lines indicate team movement. Don't advance the moving element too far or it will come into the line of fire of the fire-base element.

remains in place while the other team moves directly forward (movement) or attacks from the flank (maneuver).

In movement, the fire teams take turns as fire-base and moving elements. After moving forward, Team B stops and becomes the fixed base of fire while Team A moves up past them. The men move forward either by crawling or rushing short distances, depending on enemy fire. Leapfrogging continues until both teams are close enough to assault the enemy position.

In maneuver, Team A remains as the fire base until Team B's flanking fire disrupts the enemy enough that both teams can move in for the assault. The rifle platoon attacks in the same way as the squad: the three squads take turns as fire-base and moving elements, or two can remain as fire base while the third maneuvers. Do *not* use double envelopment (pincers move), because it is difficult to control and often results in friendly forces firing on each other.

The purpose of infantry is to close with the enemy to capture or destroy him. The unit leader makes the decision to assault based on the enemy's fighting condition and proximity (normally within 50 yards). After completing the assault, either consolidate the position by digging in or move away using march tactics. Although daytime frontal attacks may inflict substantial casualties on the attacking force, they are usually preferable to night attacks because of the problems of control in poor visibility.

The most important factor in a successful attack is to get the men to fire and keep them firing. Experience has shown that this is a very difficult task to accomplish and one that requires firm leadership.

Brig. Gen. S.L.A. Marshall, a noted military historian and author, studied front-line warfare in World War II and concluded that only 15 percent of riflemen in action actually fired their weapons in battle. The reason? Firing means exposing your head or body, so most men hid their heads in their hands and let the firing be done by others. The thought that "if I don't fire at them, they won't fire at me" is also a contributing factor to poor fire discipline.

Rifles should be zeroed in for 200-yard range, but you should use aimed fire only while you are at rest and in the prone, sitting, or kneeling positions. When moving forward in

DOUBLE ENVELOPMENT

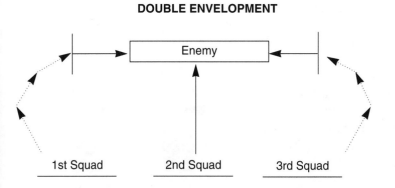

1st Squad   2nd Squad   3rd Squad

The above tactic can lead to friendly forces firing on each other and should not be attempted by small units.

RIFLE SQUAD IN DEFENSE

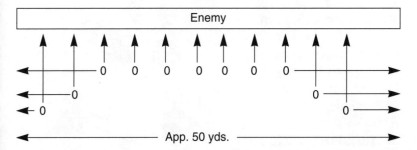

App. 50 yds.

Use 5-yard spacing between each foxhole. The foxholes at each end of the line should be dug larger to accommodate two men in order to allow reinforcements from other parts of the line if necessary. Each man's field of fire is a wide cone to his front. Do not try to obtain interlocking fire; this is effective only with machine guns.

a standing position, as in the assault phase of the attack, all fire should be by instinctive pointing, with rifles held at waist level and eyes focused on the target. No one can align sights properly when walking rapidly, and if the men stop to aim, the momentum of the assault will be lost.

Be sure to keep the fire-base elements firing while the moving or maneuvering elements are in motion; such firing tends to keep the enemy heads down, thus reducing return fire. The hit rate of rifle fire in modern armies is estimated at less than 5 percent, so if you can get your men to fire at all—and then to fire with some accuracy—you will have really achieved something. Poor marksmanship has plagued armies for a long time, as evidenced at the Battle of Rosebud Creek in Montana on June 16, 1876, when U.S. Gen. George Crook's men fired some 25,000 rounds and hit only 99 Native Americans— 252 rounds per hit!

Defensive Tactics

Defend on high ground if possible, but do not dig in on the highest part of the ground, thus silhouet-

HAND SIGNALS

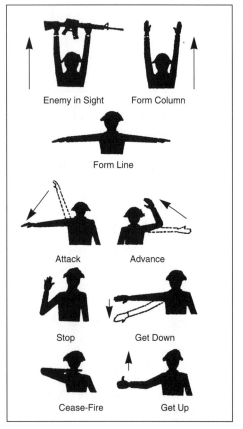

Enemy in Sight | Form Column

Form Line

Attack | Advance

Stop | Get Down

Cease-Fire | Get Up

ting your men against the skyline. Form your main line of resistance (MLR) on ground that gives good fields of fire as well as an escape route for withdrawal. Ground that allows grazing fire (fire whose trajectory is parallel to the ground), such as a gentle slope, is better than high points that permit plunging fire only (fire whose trajectory is at an angle to the ground).

A squad should deploy on one line, with foxholes staggered at both ends of the line to allow fire to both the front and flanks. A platoon can deploy with all men on one line or can keep one squad in reserve (dug in behind the MLR) to be used against flank or rear attacks or to reinforce the main line if there is a breakthrough. Because paramilitary platoons normally operate as independent units, we recommend all squads deploy on one line with end squads using staggered foxholes to protect the flanks.

Do *not* use outposts as they will be destroyed piecemeal. Keep all men on or behind the MLR.

When you withdraw, do so by echelon, with elements of your force taking turns with covering fire until all troops are withdrawn. Defensive tactics should always be viewed as a temporary expedient by any unit operating alone. Do *not* allow yourself to be pinned down; withdraw as soon as possible. After withdrawal, march tactics are reinstituted.

CONCLUSION

By training in the small-unit tactics covered here your units will improve over time. If units should merge to form larger units, such as companies or battalions, they should use the same tactics. The larger the unit, the more vital communications become, either with radios or with runners, to control and coordinate.

You will normally use offensive tactics only against an inferior force (except for hit and run). Use defensive tactics against a superior force and then withdraw. Do not counterattack; you risk being drawn into a trap.

To be a successful tactician, keep in mind these three principles of war used by the French army: (1) concentration of force, (2) liberty of action, (3) surprise. Finally, give heed to the U.S. Army's axiom: "A poor plan well executed is far better than the best plan poorly executed."

One last note: some of the best information about infantry tactics can be found in the manual *An Infantryman's Guide to Combat in Built-Up Areas*, available from Paladin Press.

CHAPTER 7

CLEARING BUILDINGS

If a suspect can't be talked into coming out of a building and chemical munitions haven't worked, more than likely an entry team will have to go in and bring the suspect out or rescue any hostages.

At least one SWAT or MOUT team of four to five men will be needed, depending on the size of the building and the number of suspects. Additionally, sniper/countersnipers will need to be set up outside the building as well as other officers to apprehend any suspects who may attempt to escape while your entry team is inside. Prior to attempting any building-clearing operations, you should evacuate adjoining buildings as well as any structures behind and across the street from your target. This is a good time to put your reserve officers to work and keep curious onlookers at a safe distance.

Part of your intelligence gathering should include a city block diagram (see sample). By plotting where your target building is on this diagram and identifying any other nearby buildings, you get a tactical overview of the entire area. On the sample diagram, we have listed some of the important intelligence information you'll want to include. Depending on the area and terrain, you may wish to include other information such as alleyways, gangways, or yards. Plotting out the area ensures that you'll have all buildings cleared of innocent civilians prior to any assaults. Additionally, you'll have an overview of any possible escape routes and have them all covered.

Your next step prior to entry will be to collect all the information possible about the actual building itself. Is it a single- or multistory dwelling? Or is it a multistory department store that occupies an entire city block or a simple one-story warehouse? You don't have to be an engineer or artist to draw a sketch of the targeted building. Plain typing paper, pencil, eraser, and ruler are all you need to plot the floor plan of a building. Be sure to identify all doorways, windows, light switches, closets, stairwells, storage rooms, and other notable features on your diagram. You can never have too much information on hand prior to making an entry. Our illustration is of a typical single-story, single-family dwelling.

You may wish to include an exploded diagram as part of your intelligence gathering. This type of diagram gives you a more precise look at what is contained on each wall.

CITY BLOCK DIAGRAM

Arrow to North

Scene Address _____ Type Building _____
Frame, brick, etc.

Used As _____ By _____
Home, type business, etc.   Lessee or owner

Owner _____ Insurance _____ Amt. $ ____
In fire cases

Neighborhood _____ Street Lighting _____
Business, residential, poor, etc.

Type Streets _____ Type Alley _____

Symbols or Comments: _____

SAMPLE SKETCH OF TARGETED BUILDING

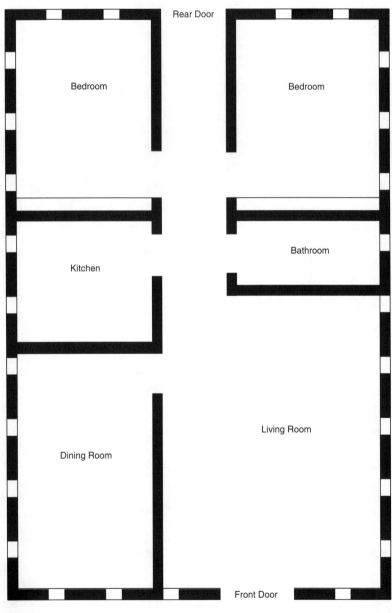

SAMPLE EXPLODED VIEW OF ROOM

Arrow to North

Address_____ Owner_____ Leasee _____

Room Located in _____ Adjoining _____ Used for _____

Walls_____ Floor _____ Ceiling _____
       Composition, Color   Bare, Carpeted, Etc.   Composition, Color

Lamps and Lights _____ Switch_____
            Location, and if Functional   Location, and if Functional

Entrance and Exits _____

Symbols or Comments: _____

An unusual problem: which door should be entered first?

A hospital would be a SWAT team's worst nightmare to clear. There are too many floors with numerous rooms, each filled with sick or injured people whose safety must be of utmost importance.

Retail stores present a lot of obstacles to teams attempting to clear them. Racks of clothing and outdoor equipment in this military-surplus store (above) or rows of large appliances in this furniture store (below) provide the bad guys with a lot of places to hide.

SWAT team making a forced entry into a building. (Photo courtesy of Michael's of Oregon.)

There are a number of methods for assaulting or entering a building. The preferred method, and the one we teach, is that a building should be cleared from the top floor, back to front, and then to the lower floors, back to front (if possible). Each building will have its own particular set of circumstances, and you may have to alter the way you will enter and clear it. Make sure you have a plan *before* attempting an entry.

If your target building is in a busy metropolitan area, you should be able to advance on it fairly easily without being

SWAT members rappelling down a building. This is an advanced technique.

Stairwells are a killer's battlefield. Move up or down them quickly.

Hallways "canalize" your movements. Get through them as quickly as possible.

observed. However, if it is in a rural area or an industrial-type park, you will want to mask your entry team's approach with a heavy smoke screen. Don't be tight-fisted here; smoke grenades are cheap insurance to cover your team's movement. Keep in mind, however, that smoke merely conceals— it is *not* a cover against bullets. Make your approach as a team: everyone should know your destination prior to moving, and you should proceed quickly and silently.

Once you have reached your target, you'll have to make your entry. Depending on the size and number of stories of your targeted building, you'll have to decide on where your point of entry will be. If it is a simple, single-floor building, your decision will be easy. If it is a multistory building, your decision will be much harder. Will you need a ladder, ropes, or grappling hooks to breach the building? In the event it is a high-rise building, you may even have to be lifted by helicopter to the roof and rappel your way down from there. Prior to making any entry into your targeted building, you'll want to have the suspect(s) occupied elsewhere if possible. This is where your negotiator will come in handy. Otherwise, you'll have to feign some type of distraction to draw the suspect's attention away from the point of entry. If all else fails, you'll want to deploy "flash-bang" grenades to stun the suspect, thus giving you every possible advantage and reducing police and civilian casualties.

There are two schools of thought as how best to conduct your room-by-room building clearing once you have made your entry. One school contends that it should be done silently, the other that your team should make as much noise as possible, thus alerting the suspect that you are inside and maybe scaring him into surrendering. You must set up your own particular set of guidelines about this type of movement. We teach the silent method but have no problem with the noise method. If you are employing flash-bang grenades when clearing each room, you are obviously using the noise method.

When entering through a door, enter on the correct side, not on the wrong side as this fellow is.

Do not raise your gun in the "Hollywood" style when entering through a door. If you do, the suspect may grab it.

Once your entry team is inside, you'll want to avoid spending much time in hallways or stairwells. They are killing zones for the suspect, because your movement in these areas is limited and you are "canalized." Two men should be used to clear a stairwell. If clearing from top to bottom, one man should stay at the top landing while the other proceeds down the stairs. When clearing bottom to top, one should be stationed at the bottom while the other works his way up to the top. When going up or down stairs, stay as close to the wall as possible so you're not standing dead center in the stairwell. Additionally, when moving down a hallway, your entire team should stay against one side of the hallway.

When you have a four-to-five-man entry team, your point-man should lead the way while the next two to three team members actually clear the room, followed by your rear-guard team member. Your point man and rear-guard man are exactly that: they protect your team's forward and rear elements from surprise attack. When you approach your target room, your point man should be to one side of the doorway (*always*) looking toward the front, and your room assault team should be to the other side of the door, backed up by the rear-guard man (*always*), looking toward the rear. Never mind what you may have seen in the movies, where two men stand on the sides of a door and when they enter the room they crisscross each other. It sure looks impressive on the big screen; however, it will get you killed in real life! Crisscrossing in front of each other not only exposes one or both men to each other's weapons, it is also time consuming and confusing.

PROBABLE CONCEALMENT AREAS

- Bedrooms—behind doors, inside closets or on a closet shelf, behind or under a bed, or behind or under a dresser.
- Living rooms—behind doors, behind or under a sofa or tables, inside fireplace or piano.

Keep your gun down near your waist, close to your body (above), or at the low-ready position (below) to prevent it from being snatched.

- Dining room—behind door, behind or under table or chest.
- Bathroom—behind door, inside bathtub or shower, behind sink or toilet, inside linen closet.
- Porch—behind door, behind or under furniture.
- Basement—behind doors, inside storage lockers, inside coal bin or chute, behind water heater, behind washer or dryer, inside cardboard storage boxes.
- Attic—behind door, inside rafters, behind or under furniture, inside cardboard storage boxes.
- Garage—behind, in, or under automobile, behind tool chest, inside cardboard storage boxes.

The above will give you just a few suggestions as to where suspects may hide. It is only limited by the person's imagination and size. A full-grown adult can easily hide under a pile of dirty clothes or a pile of blankets at the foot of the bed.

When entering a room, *never go directly through an open door!* Enter a room at a right or left angle to the door while crouching or, if necessary, somersaulting. When making an entry at night, you should have your flashlight in hand. There are a number of techniques available for using a flashlight (e.g., Harries or FBI technique). Use whatever technique you have been trained in. Turn on light switches at first if possible. Don't "throw" your flashlight into the middle of the room prior to entering. (Don't laugh; we have seen students perform this stupid act, only to find themselves without any sort of illumination because their flashlight breaks or it is out of their reach.)

Once a room has been entered and cleared, the team leader should announce it and mark the door or door frames to let other teams know the room is clear. In the past, we have used bright orange self-adhesive dots that are available from any office supply store. They peel off easily and are easy to spot. Other options are spray paint, white tape, or chalk.

If it can be positively verified which room a suspect is in, you may elect to use flash-bang grenades prior to entering. This will temporarily blind and confuse him and perhaps, just perhaps, no shots will have to be fired by your team members. If the suspect is holding hostages, you will want to be very careful when employing any pyrotechnic devices. Flash-bang grenades have been known to rupture eardrums. Again, depending on the given situation, you may elect to take the suspect out by using your sniper/countersniper or, as some law enforcement departments refer to them, police marksman. Taking out the suspect by this means eliminates the high risk involved in an entry and building-clearing operation during a crisis. Of course, this isn't always possible, and you may well have to go in after a suspect.

Another handy device for room clearing is the chemical light stick. You simply bend it and shake up the solution, and you then have instant light. There are some light sticks on the market that "burn" for approximately 30 minutes with a very high intensity; these are the ones you'll want to use. One reason for employing artificial light is, of course, to illuminate the room prior to entering. Another reason is that it tends to confuse the suspect. He may try to retrieve the light source and use it against you. If this is done, you know for sure that you have a suspect in that room. Another valid reason for using light sticks is that with them there is no chance of fire or injury like there is with flash-bang grenades. Some brands of flash-bang grenades have been known to have secondary "missiles" from the grenade casing that caused serious injury.

When clearing buildings and rooms, always be on the lookout for booby traps that may have been set. As part of every training exercise we put on, we routinely place a number of booby traps throughout the building. These range from simple smoke grenades to fish line with weights (not hooks, as a suspect or terrorist might use). We have yet to have a team go through a building without tripping at least one booby trap. If you have done your job and collected as much intelligence as is available (e.g., weapons, suspect's training and background, building's use), you can limit injuries from booby traps. If during your intelligence-gathering investigation you learn that the suspect is a former military demolition expert or highly trained terrorist, you might well be advised to walk softly and keep a close eye out for explosive-type booby traps.

As every SWAT call-out presents very high risks (remember, no "gee whiz" operations), it is smart to have an ambulance and paramedics standing by. However, in the event an officer is injured while clearing a building, you obviously can't have the paramedic crew enter the house and administer first aid. So as part of every team member's training, first aid is a must. Needless to say, you should have your first-aid kit on hand and not back at the command post.

Be advised that hostage takers and terrorists have been known to switch clothes with their hostages and even place unloaded weapons in their hostages hands. If any person is encountered during your building search, he must be treated as a suspect and restrained accordingly until his identity can be established. Also, if a hostage has spent any amount of time with his captors, he may have been brainwashed or at the very least become sympathetic to the hostage taker's plight. A sad story goes a long way in convincing someone to cooperate with his abductor. Many hostages have taken the side of their captors after spending time with them and listening to how bad their lives have been, or why they have to do what they are doing. This is known as the Helsinki Syndrome.

Before closing this chapter, we want to stress training once again. Your team should get together at least once a month for a serious building-clearing operation. This will involve obtaining the use of various buildings (either public or private) for your entry training techniques. Be aware that you will *not* want to use any type of smoke or incendiary-type booby traps during these training exercises, unless you are using a large vacant building and the chance of fire is slim to none. Have the local fire department standing by in the event of fire during your training exercises. Use your imagination when designing booby traps. Sometimes it will be a no-win situation for the officers, and other times the operation will go smooth as silk. Play it both ways for realism. In the past, we have used young children in the building (playing the part of the suspect), without telling the entry team about it. You'll be surprised how many officers are shot (with a blank gun) by these seemingly innocent children who they thought were simply playing in the building. Of course, when conducting these types of training exercises, it is important that no firearms be allowed on team members. A realistic substitute is the now popular paintball guns. It gets the ol' heart to pounding when you are shot with one of these nonguns. It drives home the point better than anything else we have seen or used.

CHAPTER 8

IT'S A BOMB!

Originally, it was not our intent to include this particular topic in this book. However, with the bombings of the World Trade Center in New York and the federal building in Oklahoma City, we thought that we should at least touch on the subject. Although most major metropolitan areas have their own explosive ordnance departments, the small-town police or rural sheriff's departments or paramilitary units don't have this luxury. So we'll briefly cover this subject and direct you to the proper agency that can assist if your SWAT or paramilitary unit is unfortunate enough to run across a bomb or bomb scare.

Bombs are a favorite way of eliminating people. Every terrorist organization in the world uses bombs (it's their preferred method of assassination). It is not unheard of these days to run across crude a black-powder pipe bomb or fertilizer-diesel fuel mixture (ANFO) bomb that some deranged person has left in a building, car, or wastebasket, or even a high-tech bomb placed by a terrorist in a department store. Either way, *don't touch it* unless you have been trained in explosive ordnance devices (EOD) by the military or other similar agency. The worst thing you can do is touch anything that even remotely looks like an explosive device. Leave it alone, and let the experts handle it.

Most phone calls to large corporations or police departments claiming that a bomb has been planted are false alarms. However, you must obtain as much information as possible from the caller about the bomb threat. You should ask when the bomb is set to go off, what type of a bomb it is, and where it is. Never evacuate the entire building needlessly. This may be exactly what a terrorist wants. By evacuating the entire building, you may be exposing yourself and the occupants to an assassin's bullet or, worse, exposing them to the place where the bomb has actually been placed.

After a bomb threat has been received by your department or unit, every department head involved should search his area of responsibility. No one is better equipped to search your office, car, or building than you. There is a preferred method to searching, one that is used by the U.S. Secret Service. A room should be searched (visually) from top to bottom. Not all at once, mind you; the room should be divided into three sections. The top section of the room should be searched first, then the middle, and finally the lower portion. If you find something out of place, *don't touch it!* Notify whoever is in command and get EOD personnel to check it out.

If a bomb is found, there is still no need to evacuate the entire building. Any bomb that can be hand-carried into a building will command a small explosive effect and will not destroy an entire building. As a rule, a few floors above and below the bomb and several offices to the left and right of the

AREAS TO SEARCH IN AN AUTOMOBILE

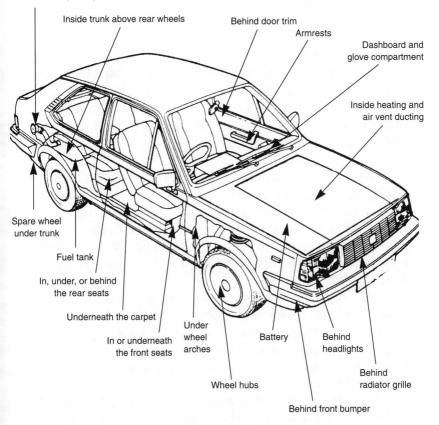

Trunk floor, especially sides

Inside trunk above rear wheels

Behind door trim

Armrests

Dashboard and glove compartment

Inside heating and air vent ducting

Spare wheel under trunk

Fuel tank

In, under, or behind the rear seats

Underneath the carpet

In or underneath the front seats

Under wheel arches

Battery

Behind headlights

Behind radiator grille

Wheel hubs

Behind front bumper

bomb should be evacuated. This is especially important if you are called to a large office building where there may be several thousand employees. It is not feasible to move that many people safely, and, as already mentioned, you may be doing exactly what the caller wants: moving people toward a bomb instead of away from it.

Though North America hasn't been plagued by car bombs as much as European and Middle Eastern countries have, the threat is there. And, while an unattended briefcase bomb is severely limited in its destructive capacity, a car or truck bomb can be devastating.

If the maker of a suspected car bomb is available, have him accompany you (under close guard) while you inspect the car or truck it is implanted on. It is highly unlikely he will want to be blown up by his own devices. However, there are some radical terrorist groups who think nothing of dying for their cause, so please exercise caution.

There are a good number of areas within an automobile where a bomb can be placed (just ask U.S. Customs agents, who search thousands of vehicles a day for drugs). The accompanying illustration shows the most likely places a bomb might be placed in an automobile. Study it thoroughly, especially if you are assigned to protect a government witness or other VIP.

If an abandoned or parked car is suspected of containing explosives, it can very well have several hundred pounds in the trunk or, in the case of a truck, several thousand pounds of explosives (as used against the U.S. Marines in Lebanon several years ago to destroy their barracks and murder more than 200 good men).

If your department or unit doesn't have someone trained in EOD, you can contact the nearest FBI office or military base, and someone there can direct you to the proper personnel. Unfortunately, if you are in a rural area, an EOD team may be several hours away, and the timing device may be set to detonate prior to its arrival. If this is the case, evacuate the area, remain a safe distance away, and wait for help to arrive. *Again, don't try to disarm the bomb yourself—this only works in the movies!* The professionals in this field will tell you there is no safe way to disarm a bomb. The preferred method is to remove it and detonate it at a safe location.

It is a good idea to have several of your team members trained at one of the military or federal (FBI or BATF) schools in order to become grounded in the basics of explosives. If someone can't recognize the "firing train" of an explosive device, he may not know what he is looking at in the first place. The U.S. military affords you the best opportunity to train and work with all types of explosives. Unfortunately, to receive all the necessary training in this field, you would need to enlist in one of the branches of the military armed forces. This is not a viable option for most people. However, all is not lost: you can enlist for a short hitch in the National Guard or U.S. Army Reserve and go away to various schools to learn this trade without giving up your law enforcement job. Otherwise, you will want to check out the FBI and BATF courses in explosives and attend one that suits your needs. Either way, remember that there is *no safe way to disarm a bomb!* With that said, we'll close this mini-course on bombs.

CHAPTER 9

PHYSICAL CONDITIONING

Coauthor John McSweeney is 68 years old, but many people tell him that he looks closer to 48. And he moves like an athlete of 28. What's more, he expects to remain vigorous and youthful right up to the end of his days. What gives him such confidence is an exercise method he developed called Tiger Moves.

If you are chosen as a member of a SWAT or paramilitary team, you owe it to yourself and your fellow team members to maintain your readiness. By incorporating McSweeney's Tiger Moves into your daily lives, you'll find improved health, physical agility, and strength. Everyone can find the 10 minutes a day it takes to exercise using the Tiger Moves.

Pat Cascio takes no credit for the information in this chapter. It should be noted, however, that his martial arts schools use the Tiger Moves system in all their warm-up sessions because it is the best system available.

ANIMAL WISDOM

Many of the exercise systems used to stay in shape actually harm the body and hasten the aging process. Exercise machines and free weights can tear muscles, wear out joints, and damage the vascular system. Jogging, long-distance running, and aerobics can injure bones in the feet, legs, and back. These exercises can also expend energy needlessly, often in excess of the body's ability to recuperate. This overexertion eventually wears down the body, making it susceptible to infection and disease. More to the point, the wear and tear caused by these methods can make you look older than your years.

Tigers and other animals, however, use an exercise system that helps them stay in top shape throughout life, does no harm to their bodies, and keeps them young right up to the time death takes over. Humans would do well to discard their methods and follow the simple wisdom of tigers and other animals who use an innate exercise system.

This is the reason McSweeney calls his exercise system Tiger Moves. His system can produce a well-proportioned physique resembling that of a trained boxer or gymnast as well as great strength and good health. The movements energize the body and fight the aging process by increasing blood flow through the smallest capillaries, including those located in facial skin. One move, the high reach, has curative powers and can restore an injured shoulder to its normal range of movement.

These exercises require no gym or equipment, so they can be done anywhere at any time. They are far superior to weights, machines, or calisthenics, and McSweeney and his martial arts students are living proof of their effectiveness.

GREAT TENSION

What is the Tiger Moves system? Nothing more than stretching with great tension.

Watch the household cat when he stands up from sleeping. He stretches his entire body with a tension so great that his limbs actually quiver—nothing like a person's yawning stretch or a stretch to increase flexibility. Instead, the cat's stretch is so powerful it actually builds muscles. The tension is the secret. The inner resistance produced by the tension builds muscle fibers just as much as the external resistance produced by weights or machines. Since the resistance is perfectly controlled throughout the entire range of motion, no harm is done to the muscles, joints, or bones.

LEARNING FROM THE ANCIENTS

The ancient martial arts masters observed the animals to learn fighting methods, which they incorporated into their martial arts systems. They also noted the animals' methods and imitated them in tension exercises.

When McSweeney began his martial arts training in 1952, he was impressed not only with its fighting efficacy but also with its bodybuilding power. He adopted tension exercises as his primary exercise system, replacing the calisthenics that had previously kept his body muscular and strong. Eventually he altered the ancient moves, which had a limited range of movement, to those that covered a full range of motion. This alteration allowed complete expansion and contraction of opposing muscle structures, and Tiger Moves was the end result.

GETTING THE BEST BENEFITS

To get the most benefit from the exercises, keep the following information in mind.

Add Aerobic Exercise

Tiger Moves keep the entire body in shape, but we recommend adding a long walk or swimming at least twice a week.

Frequency

Tiger Moves should be done daily in three sets with 10 repetitions of each move per set.

Tension

The key to the system is the tension used in stretching. Vary the amount of tension until it feels comfortable. If you use only a small amount of tension you will maintain tone but not build muscle. Too much tension can strain tendons and ligaments and also cause headaches. After a few weeks, you will know instinctively how much tension to apply. A sufficient amount will develop the muscle fibers just as much as weight lifting, although the Tiger Moves process takes longer.

Breathing

Tiger Moves should be performed slowly, with great tension. Breathe using both nose and mouth, inhaling on the way back (or up) and exhaling on the way forward (or down).

TIGER MOVES EXERCISES

The routine is composed of seven basic techniques: barrel squeeze, shoulder roll, wrist twist, high reach, pull down, stomach roll, and knee bend.

Barrel Squeeze

Stand with your left foot one pace forward. Bend your left knee and keep your back straight. Hold your hands in front, with your palms facing up. Bring your hands back slowly, using great tension, until the back muscles are fully flexed.

Hold this position for a count of one and then move the hands forward slowly and with tension until the palms face each other. Hold this position for a count of one and then repeat the entire procedure. Be sure your arms remain parallel to the floor. The shoulders should be held naturally and not lifted. Breathe through your nose and mouth, inhaling on the way back and exhaling on the way forward. Feel the pectoral (chest) muscles working.

Shoulder Roll

Stand with your feet apart, both knees bent, and your back straight. Start with your hands in fists and both arms bent. Roll the shoulders back until the back muscles are flexed and then roll them forward until your arms cross your chest. Keep the forearms parallel to the ground and your shoulders low, not lifted. Feel the deltoid (shoulder) muscles working.

Wrist Twist

Stand with right foot one pace forward. Bend the right knee and keep your back straight. Hold your arms in front, close to your body, with fists turned in, and rotate your arms back, turning the fists gradually until they turn out. Flex the back muscles and rotate the arms forward to the starting position, turning your fists gradually until they turn in completely. Keep your arms down and close to your body during the entire movement. Feel the triceps (upper arm) working.

High Reach

Stand with your feet apart, both arms held straight up. Reach as high as possible with one arm at a time and the other arm moving down slightly each time. Breathe in and out on each count.

Pull Down

Stand with your feet apart. With hands in fists, lift one

arm slightly above your head and pull down close to the center line of the body using great tension. As you pull one arm down, move the other one up. This exercise works the inner pectorals, biceps, and forearms.

Stomach Roll
Stand with your feet apart. Press your stomach down with great tension as you exhale. Then suck the stomach in as far as possible as you inhale.

Knee Bend
Stand with your feet apart. Bend halfway only, since deep knee bends harm the joints. Be sure to maintain great tension while bending. Knee bends strengthen leg muscles and knee joints.

MUSCLE SIZE AND STRENGTH

Working out with Tiger Moves resulted in an increase in muscle size and strength far in excess of what calisthenics had previously done for McSweeney, his students, and instructors. Furthermore, McSweeney has been able to maintain a powerful physique through the years with only a minimum effort. You can get the same results with Tiger Moves.

CHAPTER 10

HAND-TO-HAND COMBAT

Nowhere is Murphy's Law—that if anything can go wrong, it will go wrong—more applicable than when you're dealing with weapons. Sooner or later your weapon is going to jam or malfunction. Just hope it doesn't happen when you're in a high-stress situation. That's why throughout this text we have repeatedly admonished you not to rely on high-tech gear or equipment. In the event something does go awry with your weapon, you'll need to fall back on your own two hands and feet to deal with the threat.

Both authors of this book are serious martial arts students (we call ourselves students because we are still learning our trade and developing and improving on time-tested hand-to-hand combat methods). We don't think any book dealing with SWAT or paramilitary training or operations is complete without some type of training in hand-to-hand combat. The following story illustrates that importance.

Two elderly gentlemen dressed in tuxedos hailed a cab outside a posh restaurant in midtown Manhattan and directed the driver to take them to Madison Square Garden. One passenger was Jack Dempsey, former heavyweight champion of the world, and the other was the New York State boxing commissioner. Completely relaxed in the back of the cab, they looked forward to attending the title fight at which they would be honored guests.

When their taxi stopped for a red light, two hoodlums wielding knives suddenly wrenched open both rear doors, leaned in, and demanded money. Without hesitation, Dempsey hit one with a left jab and the other with a right cross, and their lights went out. Two knockouts in rapid succession for the champ, who still had knockout power at the age of 70. Although Dempsey hadn't fought professionally since his mid-30s, he had never stopped training. He trained just enough to keep his muscle structure strong and his timing sharp, so it was easy to keep working out through the years. When the need for self-defense arose, he proved that a fighter can still maintain his hitting power even as he ages. Dempsey's secret was regular training.

Self-defense is for life. It is not merely a sport you engage in when you are young. The skills learned in the competitive "sport" karate are useful for lifelong self-defense as long as you continue to train regularly throughout your life.

HAND-HITTING POWER

This is easier to learn and maintain than kicking power simply because of physics. Legs are three to four times heavier than arms, so practitioners must be cautious of the wear and tear on knee and hip joints caused by kicking, especially high kicking, because it can eventually weaken the body as it ages.

Arms are shorter and lighter than legs so their muscles can move hands with lightning-quick speed and minimal wear on elbow and shoulder joints. Being able to maintain this hand speed through the years is critical because speed is vital to knockout hitting power.

Instead of going into great detail on martial arts training, we will describe nine power strikes that are effective and easy to use when the chips are down.

1. *Chop to larynx, side of neck, back of neck, and brain stem.* To perform a chop, open the hand, curl the fingers slightly, cock thumb, and bend the hand back toward the wrist. The striking surface is the meaty section at the bottom of the palm and adjacent to the wrist bone. Do not use the side of the hand as the striking surface because it will give upon impact and thus diminish the force of the blow. To chop to the right side, bring the right leg forward. If chopping to the left, lead with the left leg. Hold the hand palm up near your rib cage and then swing it forward and around in a circular motion, turning the palm down just before impact. Think of cutting right through the target and let the hand swing backward as far as it can go. Power comes from the circular movement of the hand, pulled by the shoulder and back

John McSweeney demonstrating a chop.

muscles and augmented by turning the waist. Move the body center toward the direction of the chop.

To chop downward, bring the hand back, up, and down, completing a full circle. Power comes from the shoulder and back muscles as well as the body center, which drops just as the hand hits the target. Start with wide chops to develop the muscle structure, and then work short chops with the elbow bent.

2. *Heel palm to forehead, eye socket, base of nose, and jaw.* To execute properly, curl your fingers and bend your hand back toward the wrist. The striking area is the base of the palm. Unlike with the fist, which pivots on two axes, there is no give when hitting with the heel palm, so all the force is transferred to the target. Chamber the hand near your waist, palm up, and then thrust it forward and whip it right back, getting power from the shoulder and back muscles. Simultaneously, move the body center forward. Be sure the strike is straight, with no fishtailing effect.

Leopard Palm.

3. *Leopard Palm to the bridge of nose, upper skull, and jawbone.* Curl your fingers and bend your hand back. The striking surface is the

base of the palm. This strike is like a chop, only in reverse. Power comes from the circular movement of the hand, pulled by the shoulder and back muscles and augmented by turning the waist and moving the body center down in conjunction with the strike. The hand loops up, over, and down, smashing right through the target. This is the same strike as former world heavyweight boxing champion (1952–1955) Rocky Marciano's looping right, which was responsible for most of his knockouts. He normally hit the skull or jawbone and, occasionally, broke his thumb because, as a boxer, he hit with a clenched fist.

4. *Eagle's Claw to larynx.* This weapon is formed by the thumb and index finger. Strike forward like a snake and grab the back of the larynx, behind the thyroid cartilage. Squeeze the two fingers together to control and immobilize. Maintaining the tight squeeze and pulling back rapidly destroy the breathing structure and cause almost instant death. Develop squeeze power by opening and closing your thumb and fingers, using great tension, at least 200 times per day.

Side fist.

5. *Fingers and thumb.* Poke and

scratch eyeballs and grab testicles. Poke with your thumb, index finger, or two fingers. When using thumb or index-finger strikes, be sure to support these weapons with the other fingers to avoid injuring them. Practice fast, short, straight strikes and then work circular strikes with the five fingers held like a tiger's claw. Practice opening and closing the fingers and hand to develop grabbing strength.

6. *Side fist to heart and jawbone.* The striking surface is the middle knuckle. Power comes from driving the hand forward like a battering ram, using force from the shoulder and getting torque as you hit. Holding the fist sideways instead of turning it down keeps the elbow tucked in, thus maintaining alignment of the fist, wrist, and forearm with the shoulder. This produces a pile-driver effect, which makes this strike far more powerful than a boxer's right cross. It is known as the "heart-stop" punch and can easily break the sternum.

7. *Upswing to jawbone.* The striking surface is the middle knuckle, so be sure to bend the hand back on the wrist before impact to avoid breaking bones on the top of the hand. Power comes from the shoulder as the hand

Looping elbow.

moves forward, up, and back to its starting position, completing a full circle. Moving the body center up simultaneously with the strike adds to the power. This strike is very fast and has triple the force of a boxer's uppercut. It will easily break the jawbone. If you miss this target, continue the swing to strike the pubic bone or bladder area.

8. *Elbow to the jawbone, upper skull, and rib cage.* This is the body's second most powerful natural weapon (after the knee) and can be used to hit forward, backward, up, and down. The forward, looping elbow strike moves forward, up, over, and down, driving through the upper skull or jawbone. The power comes from the elbow's circular movement, augmented by the shoulder, back, and waist turn. To gain more power, drop the body center down and in the same direction as the elbow. This blow can easily knock out the largest opponent.

9. *Knee to the pubic bone, bladder, and testicles.* Practice driving the knee up as fast as possible and then practice driving it forward. Keep the calf and thigh as close together as possible to get maximum weight behind the knee. The jumping knee is an offensive tactic with tremendous force. Jump forward on one foot and smash the opposite knee straight into the pubic bones. The entire body weight moving forward adds greatly to the power. The knee is the body's heaviest weapon and can easily break the weak pubic bones at their juncture or rupture the bladder.

We believe that the above nine power strikes are the most effective and easily learned (and maintained) self-defense techniques for SWAT, paramilitary, or civilian use.

Traditional martial arts training is no longer geared for street combat. The unarmed self-defense techniques developed by the early martial artists have long since been revamped and geared toward competition rather than real-life threats. (Of course, there are exceptions to every rule, and in the Appendix we'll list some martial arts schools that provide training in knockout power as well as serious self-defense techniques that work.)

Many martial arts schools train in a single form, relying on techniques that are no longer viable for life-threatening situations. For example, most karate styles train in linear movements, kung-fu stylists train in circular movements, and taekwon do stylists train in high kicks. The authors have taken what they consider the best techniques from many styles and combined them into a highly effective self-defense system. We stress training that combines circular and linear movements as well as knockout power. If a martial arts school is geared toward competition training, avoid it. A SWAT call-out is not competition. It is a deadly threat, and there's no referee on hand to make sure all parties involved are playing by the rules.

We believe that the following comparison best illustrates this point. Rocky Marciano was considered the hardest hitter of his time. But because his reach was only 67 inches, the shortest of all heavyweight champions, he had to rely on circular power (similar to Chinese kung-fu styles) to produce results. He closed rapidly and then let loose with a barrage of hooks, roundhouse swings, and one unconventional blow he introduced to boxing: the looping right. Seeming to come from nowhere, it looped up, over, and down before landing on the opponent's temple or jaw. This high-arcing blow was responsible for the majority of his knockouts.

Jack Dempsey, on the other hand, specialized in linear blows. Most of his knockouts were caused by his right cross, but he also had the rare ability to knock someone out with his left jab. In today's boxing world, this would be very rare, since most left jabs are merely flicks thrown with the back of the hand. But Dempsey threw his jab with a powerful snap, hitting full force with the knuckles while he stepped forward simultaneously with his left foot, adding body momentum to the punch's power. He called this blow his *step jab*.

We don't boast that our martial art styles are the best or the only ones you should train in. Any instructor of armed or unarmed self-defense techniques who makes such claims should be avoided at all costs. We do believe that our systems provide some of the mechanics mentioned above—knockout power and linear and circular movements—as well as training in the Tiger Moves. This isn't idle speculation on our part. The time-proven (and street-proven) mechanics of power combined with linear and circular movements is well documented by actual street combat.

Train for hitting power now and throughout the rest of your life; then use it properly. Gain this power and train moderately on a regular basis to maintain it.

We can't emphasize too strongly the need to prepare and train for the worst possible scenario: your firearm malfunctioning or jamming, your dropping it or having it taken from you, or your missing a close shot and then being forced to defend yourself with nothing more than your bare hands. If you haven't trained for these sorts of problem, you won't win. Your life—and perhaps that of an innocent hostage—may depend on how you train and react to these very real threats.

CONCLUSION

No single book can possibly cover every aspect of organizing, staffing, training, equipping, and operating a SWAT, MOUT, or paramilitary team, but we hope you have found the material in this book helpful.

Earlier we talked about SWAT teams that are nothing but "gee whiz" operations. We sincerely hope you heed our advice and seek the necessary training to hone your skills in this highly specialized field and avoid falling into this trap. Just reading this book—or any book for that matter—isn't enough. You need to get out there and train on a regular basis.

This book is not meant to be the final word. It is only meant to ground you in the basics. As in anything else, if you are not grounded in the fundamentals, all else is folly. Therefore, we have presented some basic military training doctrines that are easily adapted to SWAT or paramilitary operations. It would be impossible for us to lay out the complete groundwork and every possible training scenario. Take what we have presented and adapt it to fit your needs, terrain, climate, situation, personnel, and guidelines.

We strongly suggest that you purchase, read, and study some of the military and police training books and manuals available from Paladin Press. By doing this and constantly adding new material to your library, you'll soon have all the information needed to operate as the elite SWAT and military units do.

Finally, remember that this is all about teamwork and regular training and practice.

RESOURCES

In the text, we touched briefly on some of the firearms, equipment, gear, and training necessary to carry out a successful SWAT or paramilitary operation. In this section we will detail some of the resources and equipment available. This list is not all-inclusive, nor is it intended to be. We've simply listed the products and companies we are familiar with and therefore feel comfortable recommending. Most large metropolitan police and sheriff's departments are flooded daily with catalogs and brochures, all seeking to sell them new equipment. The smaller and rural departments and paramilitary units are usually left out in the cold because their purchasing power isn't comparable to that of their larger counterparts, and many companies simply are not interested in their limited business. All of the companies we list here will be happy to supply your needs.

GUNS

Although there are numerous firearms companies, we will not list all of them. We will, however, inform you of some of the better ones that are producing fine products and are willing to work with you to ensure that your department or unit will get the right weapons to carry out its assignment. You can count on their products to see you through the hardest of times.

Beretta U.S.A. Corp.
Beretta Drive
Accokeek, MD 20607
Semiautomatic handguns and shotguns suitable for law enforcement and paramilitary use. Beretta produces the Model 92 9mm semiautomatic pistol that was adopted by the U.S. military 10 years ago to replace the Colt Government Model .45 ACP.

Browning Firearms
Route One
Morgan, UT 84050-9749
Handguns suitable for law enforcement, self-protection, and paramilitary use. This company produces the Browning Hi-Power pistol in 9mm and .40 S&W caliber. At one time, various police and military forces in more than 90 countries used the Hi-Power.

Colt Manufacturing Company, Inc.
P.O. Box 1868
Hartford, CT 06144-1868
Colt produces revolvers, semiautomatic pistols, rifles, and carbines suitable for law enforcement, paramilitary, military, and self-protection needs. The AR-15 (M16 military version) is an excellent battle rifle with parts available all over the world.

Eagle Arms, Inc.
131 East 22nd Avenue
Coal Valley, IL 61240

Eagle Arms produces an excellent Colt AR-15 clone semiautomatic rifle and carbine. Tight fitting and terrific accuracy.

Glock, Inc.
P.O. Box 369
Smyrna, GA 30081

Semiautomatic pistols suitable for law enforcement, paramilitary, military, and self-defense needs. Also available to law enforcement and military only is a select-fire 9mm pistol.

Heckler & Koch, Inc.
21480 Pacific Boulevard
Sterling, VA 22170

Semiautomatic pistols, rifles, shotguns, and submachine guns suitable for law enforcement, military, and self-protection use.

O.F. Mossberg & Sons
7 Grasso Avenue
Box 497
No. Haven, CT 06473

Pump-action and semiautomatic shotguns for law enforcement, military, paramilitary, and self-protection use. Terrific prices.

Novak's .45 Shop
P.O. Box 4045
Parkersburg, WV 26104

Wayne Novak and his staff are custom gunsmiths. His guns are in use by elite law enforcement and military units all around the world. Highly recommended.

Rock Island Armory
911 West Main St.
Geneseo, IL 61254
Full-auto rifles, machine guns, and carbines suitable for law enforcement and military use.

Smith & Wesson
2100 Roosevelt Avenue
Springfield, MA 01102
Semiautomatic pistols and revolvers of all configurations suitable for law enforcement, military, paramilitary, self-protection, and sporting purposes.

Springfield Armory
420 West Main St.
Geneseo, IL 61254
Semiautomatic pistols for law enforcement, self-protection, and military use. Its 1911A1 and PDP line of pistols are recommended highly.

Sturm, Ruger & Co.
Ruger Road
Prescott, AZ 86301-6105
Semiautomatic pistols, revolvers, semiautomatic rifles, bolt-action rifles, and submachine guns all suitable for law enforcement, paramilitary, and military use. Good prices and quality.

Taurus International
161 NW 49th Avenue
Miami, FL 33014
Semiautomatic pistols and revolvers suitable for law enforcement, self-protection, and military use. Extremely good prices.

FIREARMS AND SELF-DEFENSE TRAINING

This area is generally neglected by law enforcement departments, which have their once or twice yearly qualification shoot and forgo any type of regular practice. We assume that if you are reading this book you are interested in obtaining training beyond that offered by the police academy, your department, military, or paramilitary unit.

There are any number of big-name training schools out there, but not all of the good instructors advertise in national publications. They are content to work with smaller groups of officers, civilians, and military personnel to ensure better and more individualized training. Although this list is small and certainly not all-inclusive, it does include some of the better combat firearms instructors available. We don't believe you'll be let down by their training courses. Additionally, we have listed our training schools and make no apologies because we believe we offer some of the best close-combat firearms training around.

Academy of Self-Defense
Bradley Steiner
7407 25th Avenue, NE
Seattle, WA 98115
Personalized, one-on-one training in firearms and self-defense techniques. Highly recommended and acclaimed by law enforcement and special forces personnel.

Calibre Press, Inc.
666 Dundee Road
Suite 1607
Northbrook, IL 60062-2727
Specialized training seminars on all types of officer-survival techniques.

Combat Martial Arts Academy
Pat Cascio
P.O. Box 592
Ontario, OR 97914
Close-combat handgun training specializing in point shooting and tactical shooting classes. Also, self-defense classes and seminars as well as SWAT training classes.

Defense Training International, Inc.
John S. Farnam
P.O. Box 665
Niwot, CO 80544
John Farnam is considered the "dean of tactics" in handgun, rifle, and shotgun training. His training is highly recommended.

McSweeney's Self-Defense School
John McSweeney
350 N. York Road
Elmhurst, IL 60126
Close-combat handgun training specializing in point shooting and hand-to-hand combat training and SWAT techniques.

John Perkins
132 High Avenue
Nyack, NY 10960
Serious combat handgun training as well as martial arts.

School of Self-Defense
Mark Bryans
22 Kijidava
Prescott, AZ 86301
For serious, no-nonsense self-defense training, Mark Bryans is one of the instructors you'll want to contact in the Southwest.

United States Marksmanship Academy
James R. Jarrett
1950 W. Kristal Way
Phoenix, AZ 85027

James Jarrett was mentioned earlier in this book as a SWAT authority. Contact him for training in handgun, rifle, and shotgun techniques. Highly recommended.

BODY ARMOR

We hope every law enforcement officer, military, and paramilitary member and security officer puts on his body armor before going on duty. If you don't, you're running the risk of death at the most inopportune time—*now!* SWAT, MOUT, and paramilitary units will want to look into buying body armor suitable for stopping heavy-caliber rifle and carbine rounds. If you don't, you are not serious about survival and don't belong on this type of team.

There are a number of body armor companies around; some produce excellent products, and some produce substandard vests. The companies listed below are all producing top-notch products that you can bet your life on.

American Body Armor
85 Nassau Place
P.O. Drawer 1769
Fernandia Beach, FL 32334
Body armor.

Hovey Industries, Ltd.
2793 Fenton Road
Gloucester, Ontario, Canada K1G 3N3
Body armor and riot shields.

Point Blank Body Armor
185 Dixon Avenue
Amityville, NY 11101
Body armor.

Pro-Tech Armored Products
20 Keeler Street
Pittsfield, MA 01201
Ballistic shields.

Safariland Ltd.
3120 E. Mission Boulevard
Ontario, CA 91761
Body armor and holsters.

Second Chance Body Armor
P.O. Box 578
7919 Cameron Street
Central Lake, MI 49622
Body armor with more "saves" than any other company.

AMMUNITION

Although there are a number of good ammunition companies around, we have had the distinct pleasure of testing and working with one company in particular:

Black Hills Ammunition
P.O. Box 3090
Rapid City, SD 57709
Black Hills is owned by Jeff Hoffman, a former law enforcement officer himself, so he knows your needs and produces an extensive line of high-quality ammo for all your law enforcement, paramilitary, and self-defense needs.
The Black Hills line of .223 Remington 60-grain soft-point

Black Hills Ammunition is highly recommended by the authors for all your tactical, self-defense, and target practice needs.

ammo consistently shot into 3/4-inch groups at 100 yards in an Eagle Arms Action Master rifle. You can't ask any ammo to do better than that. Black Hills handgun ammo can be counted on to get the job done as well. Drop Hoffman a line and ask for his catalog. Large and small departmental orders are accepted as well as individual orders.

HOLSTERS

The finest handgun in the world is useless without the proper rig to carry it in. We have tested and evaluated a number of holsters over the past few years and find that the following companies produce some of the best rigs around for special operations as well as for everyday duty and concealed carry use.

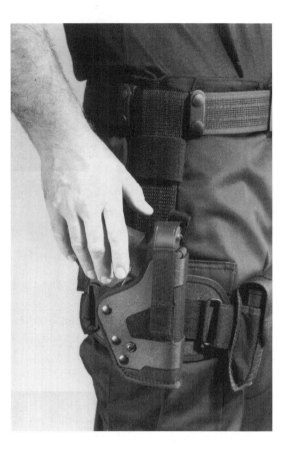

The superb Tacttical Thigh holster from Michael's of Oregon is the best rig on the market for SWAT or paramilitary use.

Bianchi International
100 Calle Cortez
Temecula, CA 92390
Full line of duty, off-duty, tactical, concealed carry, and sporting holsters.

Ted Blocker Holsters
14787 SE 82nd Drive
Clackamas, OR 97015
Custom holster maker that knows your needs and has good prices and reasonable delivery times.

Michael's of Oregon
P.O. Box 13010
Portland, OR 97213
Full line of duty, off-duty, and sporting holsters made of ballistic nylon or Michael's new Mirage line made with Nytek. Its Tactical Thigh rig is probably the best on the market.

MISCELLANEOUS GEAR AND NEEDS

While equipping your team, we hope you'll consider some of the following companies and products for those miscellaneous items you'll find you need.

Advanced Materials Laboratory, Inc.
70–90 Austin Street
Suite 205
Forest Hills, NY 11375
Tear gas delivery systems.

Brigade Quartermaster
1025 Cobb International Boulevard
Kennesaw, GA 30144-4300
A complete line of SWAT and military clothing and equipment.

Centex Security
Route 20, Box 516P
San Antonio, TX 78218
Complete training and sales of attack-trained dogs and drug-detection dogs. Good prices.

Cutlery Shoppe
5461 Kendall Street
Boise, ID 83706-1248
A complete line of excellent cutlery to fill any needs. Discount prices and free catalog.

Force Resources, Inc.
4302 Henderson Boulevard
Tampa, FL 33629
Forced-entry tools and equipment.

Gerber Legendary Blades
14200 SW 72nd Avenue
P.O. Box 23088
Portland, OR 97223
Good variety of knives that every team member should consider.

Kigre, Inc.
100 Marshland Road
Hilton Head, SC 29928
Night vision equipment.

Kwik-Vu
P.O. 2099
Warminster, PA 18974
Telescoping mirrors that come in handy when looking around corners, over walls, and into rooms without exposing yourself to gunfire.

Laseraim Technologies
P.O. Box 3548
Little Rock, AR 72203
This firm produces one of the smallest handgun laser sights on the market, and it has a quick turnaround time.

Laser Products
18300 Mt. Baldy Circle
Fountain Valley, CA 92708
An extensive line of laser sights for all types of firearms.

B.E. Meyers & Co.
17525 NE 67th Court
Redmond, WA 98052
Top-notch night vision equipment.

NVEC
P.O. Box 266
Emmaus, PA 18049
Night vision equipment.

Paladin Press
P.O. Box 1307
Boulder, CO 80306
Complete library of training manuals and books for law enforcement, security, and military personnel.

Prime Lasertech Inc.
P.O. Box 19589-498
Irvine, CA 92763
This company offers a video periscope that would be handy for looking around corners, over walls, and into rooms without exposing yourself to gunfire.

U.S. Cavalry Store
2855 Centennial Avenue
Radcliff, KY 40160-9000
Complete line of SWAT and military clothing and equipment.

W.S. Darley & Co.
2000 Anson Drive
Melrose Park, IL 60160
Police supply catalog with every type of uniform and equipment any agency can use.

As already mentioned, this list is not all-inclusive, but the companies listed above offer quality equipment, firearms, knives, clothing, books, and just about anything your SWAT or paramilitary team might need. We have used their products and give them our highest recommendation.

ABOUT THE AUTHORS

Several years ago, Pat Cascio and John McSweeney were introduced to each other by Bradley Steiner. A strong professional and personal relationship developed, and they decided to combine their experience, knowledge, and training in the armed/unarmed fields to teach point-shooting skills. An exchanging of ideas, letters, and phone calls followed. The result is this book.

Pat Cascio has spent more than 20 years in private and public law enforcement work in such capacities as private investigator, intelligence officer, police officer, city marshal, deputy sheriff, SWAT instructor, K-9 handler/trainer, security consultant, and firearms instructor/consultant.

He currently makes his living as a firearms instructor/consultant. He is a certified sixth-degree black belt in American (combat) karate and also holds a third-degree black belt in American kenpo karate. Cascio also operates two martial arts schools in eastern Oregon. His military background is in infantry tactics, leadership, and sniper training. He is a much-sought-after instructor and consultant in the armed/unarmed self-defense fields. He is the author of four books and numerous magazine articles dealing with firearms, tactics, survival techniques, and martial arts.

John McSweeney is a tenth-degree karate black belt and the founder of karate in Ireland. He spent 12 years in the U.S. armed forces, saw combat in the Korean War, and attained the rank of captain, infantry. He also served in the U.S. Border Patrol.

He presently teaches karate and handgun point shooting and works as a private investigator. His academic credentials include a bachelor's degree from St. John's University, New York City, and a master's degree from Trinity College, Dublin, Ireland.

He is the author of *Battleaxe—A Warrior's Tale* as well as numerous magazine articles on martial arts, firearms, and survival.